THE BOLSHOI

Boris Alexandrovich Pokrovsky
and Yuri Nikolayevich Grigorovich

THE BOLSHOI

Opera and Ballet at the
Greatest Theater in Russia

PARK LANE
New York

THE BOLSHOI

Editor:
FRANCESCA AGOSTINI

Design:
BRUNO ACQUALAGNA

Translated from the Russian and Italian
BY DARYL HISLOP

Photographs copyright © 1976 by Planeta
International edition copyright © 1978 by
Mondadori-Planeta-Mladinska Knjiga
English translation copyright © 1979 by Arnoldo
Mondadori Editore, S.p.A., Milano

This edition is published by Park Lane, a division
of Crown Publishers, Inc.

a b c d e f g h

Library of Congress Catalog Card Number 79-87899

Printed and bound in Italy by Officine Grafiche di
Arnoldo Mondadori Editore, Verona

Library of Congress Cataloging in Publication Data

Pokrovskii, Boris Aleksandrovich.
  The Bolshoi.

  1. Bol' shoi teatr SSSR. 2. Opera—Moscow.
3. Ballet. I. Grigorovich, IUrii Nikolaevich,
1927—   . II. Title.
ML1741.8.M72G763 1981   782.1'0947'312   81-4934
ISBN 0-517-344513   AACR2

Contents

TO THE
BOLSHOI THEATER COMPANY

Dear Comrades

All over the country we are celebrating the two hundredth anniversary of the Bolshoi Theater. I am happy to present your company with the Order of Lenin, the highest order in the Soviet Union, and with it my sincere congratulations.

The Bolshoi Theater is our pride and joy. For two centuries its outstanding achievements in the arts have kept it firmly on the road to glory. The realistic traditions of our own opera and ballet have been firmly established by the production of works by Russian classical composers on its stage.

After the October Revolution, the Bolshoi Theater, enriched by the new ideas which it brought with it, entered an era of renaissance, a truly golden age. Classical music and dance had suddenly become accessible to millions of workers, and on this stage the best revolutionary characters based on heroes from our history were created—contemporary heroes in the full sense of the term.

For many generations people have flocked to the Bolshoi Theater in the quest for noble cultural values and the wealth of music from Russia and the world over. They are always delighted by the superb artistry and talent of the Bolshoi company, which reaffirms the noble ideals of our Party and people through its work. The Bolshoi Theater is a highly professional school for artistic talent from all the Union Republics. It is no accident that your theater is known as the academy of our national musical culture.

The authority of the Bolshoi Theater is widely recognized. The humanitarian and progressive ideals, the message of friendship between peoples which its art carries, meet with warm response and gratitude in the hearts of audiences the world over.

The Twenty-fifth Congress of the Communist Party laid great emphasis on the major role played by the arts in the spiritual enrichment and moral education of our people.

Allow me, my dear comrades, to express the hope that all your work will remain faithful to this ideal, will search out and uncover the heroism of today, and will stimulate peoples' creative energy, calling upon their finest and noblest sentiments.

We are sure that Soviet artists will devote their talents to the great task of educating the new man of today.

With all my heart I wish you great success and the opening up of new frontiers in your art.

Leonid Brezhnev

On March 28, 1976, the Bolshoi Theater was two hundred years old. This important anniversary was celebrated in a national holiday. The Secretary-General of the Communist Party of the Soviet Union and President of the Presidium of the Supreme Soviet of the U.S.S.R., Leonid Brezhnev, sent the above letter to the Bolshoi Theater. The letter is evidence of the cultural importance given to this theater by the Party and the peoples of the U.S.S.R.

6

Two Centuries of the Bolshoi Theater

The history of the Bolshoi Theater dates from March 28, 1776, when Prince Urusov, a great admirer of the dramatic art, obtained a government privy for the maintenance, by him alone and no one else, of all theatrical performances in Moscow for a period of ten whole years, that there might be no detriment to him. At first Urusov's troupe gave all its performances in Prince Vorontsov's mansion on Znamenka Street. To consolidate and expand his theatrical enterprise, Urusov invited the resourceful and energetic English impresario Michael E. Maddox to become the troupe's director. According to one of the conditions of his privy, Urusov had to build within five years a stone theater "with such exterior decoration that it might serve as an ornament to the city." A site for the new theater was chosen on Petrovka Street (whence its eventual name, the Petrovsky Theater) on the spot where the Bolshoi Theater now stands. Before embarking on the construction of the Petrovsky Theater, Urusov and Maddox decided to build temporary accommodation in the Stroganov mansion. In 1780, while this accommodation was under construction, the Vorontsov Theater on Znamenka Street was destroyed by fire.

Suffering heavy losses, Urusov yielded his entire share of the privy to Maddox, who with characteristic energy set about building the Petrovsky Theater to the design of an architect called Rozberg. For twenty-five years this theater, also called the Opera House, was the scene of operatic, ballet, and dramatic performances.

In October 1805 the Petrovsky Theater burned to the ground before a performance of *Nymph of the Dnieper.* In the late autumn the troupe began performing again, first in the Volkonsky house on Samotechnaya Square, then in the Pashkov mansion on Mokhovaya Street. At this time the Moscow theater was brought under the Directorate of Imperial Theaters and in April 1806 it was given new and very splendid accommodation on Arbat Street. Built by the famous architect Rossi, it became known as the Bolshoi (Big) Theater. The Arbat theater was very beautiful, ringed about with columns and with porches on all sides; the spacious area between columns, in the form of long galleries, made a convenient place for strolling. The theater opened with a performance of the prologue to *Bayan, the Russian Bard of Ancient Times.* The fire of 1812, however, destroyed this magnificent building too.

After the expulsion of the French, theatrical life in Moscow did not resume until 1814. Theatrical presentations opened in the Ap-

Detail showing the balconies and ceiling of the Bolshoi Theater.
The theater as it is today was reconstructed in 1856 according to plans prepared by A. K. Kavos, which corrected the visual and acoustic faults of the old building.

raskin house on Znamenka Street. In 1818 productions were transferred to the Pashkov mansion on the corner of Mokhovaya and Bolshaya Nikitskaya Streets, where the troupe played until 1824. The Pashkov Theater opened on August 25 with a performance of Cherubini's opera *The Water Carrier.* In 1822 construction work began on a new theater in Petrovka Street. On January 6, 1825, the Bolshoi Petrovsky Theater was opened—one of the largest in Europe and of unparalleled magnificence. It was the work of the architect Bovet, to a design by Professor A. Mikhailov. A prologue, *The Victory of the Muses,* was composed for the grand opening by the poet Mikhail Dmitriyev to music by Alexei Verstovsky and A. Alyabyev.

The opening of the Bolshoi Petrovsky Theater came almost fifty years after the Urusov troupe's first performance, which marked the beginning of a permanent musical theater in Moscow. This comparatively short period had been a time of crucially important events. The power and international prestige of the Russian state had increased immeasurably, while at the same time progressive democratic forces were developing at a swift pace.

It was the democratic tendencies of the finest sons of the Russian intelligentsia which prepared and paved the way for the birth of a national music theater. The young theater was given an enthusiastic reception by a broadly based public.

The core of the company consisted of Urusov's serf actors, who were joined by actors from the theatrical troupes of N. Titov and Moscow University. At the Petrovsky Theater there was no division into operatic and dramatic troupes; the same actors appeared in both drama and opera. Thus we find the name of the famous tragic actor Shusherin among the first performers of the opera *The Miller-Magician, Deceiver, and Matchmaker.* This peculiarity of Russian theater continued into the first half of the nineteenth century. It is known that the outstanding Russian dramatic actors Shchepkin, Zhivokini, and others frequently performed in operas, while many opera singers, Repina, for example, successfully performed dramatic roles. Among the finest singers in the early years of the Russian stage were Sokolovskaya, Sinyavskaya, Ozhogin, and Zlov. A little later the stage of the Petrovsky Theater was frequently graced with the talent of the renowned Sandunova, a former ward of the Moscow Orphanage and a pupil of Paisiello. The Petrovsky Theater troupe was frequently augmented by talented serf actors and actresses, and occasionally by entire serf theater companies purchased by the theater management from landowners.

In 1773 a ballet school was founded at the Moscow Orphanage under the direction of the ballet master M. Valberg. This was in effect the foundation of the present Moscow Academic Choreographic School. Most of the artists who had trained at the orphanage, together with the ballet school and its teaching staff, were absorbed into the company of the newly established theater. They were joined by the serf dancers of the Urusov and Golovkina troupes.

In 1806 the serf actors at the theater were given their freedom.

The repertoire of the Petrovsky Theater at this time was remarkably varied and wide. It was, however, the original works of Russian composers that formed the basic, best loved, and most often presented part of its repertoire. As early as January 1777 the first opera by a Russian composer, the music and libretto of which have been preserved, was performed on the stage of the Znamensky Theater: *Rebirth,* a comic opera in one act by Zorin. The most popular Russian comic operas on themes of everyday life were continuously in repertoire year after year. One example here is Ablesimov and Sokolovsky's famous *The Miller* (later revised by the eminent composer Fomin), which had its premiere on the Moscow stage in January 1779. The comic operas of Pashkevich— *The Misfortune with the Carriage, The Miser, St. Petersburg Bazaar—* enjoyed great success.

Interest in simple, ordinary people, their sufferings, their natural, living speech, interest in the folk song as an important means of poetic, emotional, and truthful characterization—such were the fundamental features of Russian comic opera at the end of the eighteenth century. Many of these works tell about the lot of the serfs, victims of their masters' caprices and superstitions, threatened with being sold, sent into the army, or deported into penal servitude. In the increasingly antifeudal atmosphere of the end of the century, the peasant theme, the fate of the serfs, became a subject of great topical relevance. The comic-opera genre was especially popular with democratically minded audiences. A decisive factor in the successful formation of a national repertoire was the composers' close collaboration with the great progressive writers of the day,

Above: An engraving made in 1780 shows the Petrovsky Theater; built by M. E. Maddox according to plans by Rosberg, it was completely destroyed in the fire of October 1805.
On the following pages: View at night of the front of the Bolshoi Theater before a performance.

Kniaźnin, Ablesimov, Nikolayev, Kharaskov.

Along with national operas, popular works by the greatest foreign composers of the day were also widely performed on the Moscow stage. Examples are Pergolesi, Paisiello, Cimarosa, Salieri, Grétry, Cherubini, Boieldieu.

Predominant among the first ballet productions were conventional fabulous, mythological spectacles brought in by foreign ballet masters recruited for that very purpose. However, also widely presented were ballet-divertissements based on themes from the everyday life of the people, in which folk dances were performed. They included *A Village Scene, A Village Fête, Village Pastimes,* and *Village Divertissements at Sunrise.* Ballets on contemporary themes were also put on—*The Capture of Ochakov,* for example (1792). In presenting such spectacles, the Petrovsky Theater was responding to the needs of a broad public eager to see onstage an art that was close to them, part of themselves, accessible, and their very own.

The creative principles of the Petrovsky Theater were influenced by Moscow's university and by leading progressive social thinkers who played a most active part in the life of the theater.

A characteristic feature of the old Petrovsky Theater had been the existence of a kind of artistic council attached to it that consisted of actors, dramatists, and experts in the theater. The council assigned parts and approved new productions. Democratic tendencies and open procedures had thus been the old Petrovsky Theater's most important characteristics.

However, the situation altered abruptly when the Moscow musical troupe was taken over by the Directorate of Imperial Theaters. The reactionary, conservative policies of the imperial officials, who did all they could to fence off the art of the theater from progressive social life and subordinate it to the requirements of feudal, aristocratic court art, did the Bolshoi Theater tremendous harm. Countless obstacles were placed in the way of establishing an independent national repertoire.

Progressive figures in the theater—composers, musicians, performers—now had to wage an intense and onerous struggle against the reactionary ruling circles. The well-known composer Alexey Nikolayevich Verstovsky played an especially important role in the history of the Bolshoi Theater. Together with the playwright F. Kokoshkin, he virtually ran the theater until the end of the 1840s. He proved to be a talented artist and administrator, but is mainly remembered for his active contribution to the creation of the Russian opera. Verstovsky's works all reflect his love for folklore and folk music, and his belief in their place on the Russian stage. His main task, as he saw it, was to enrich national music. His best-known opera, *The Tomb of Askold,* was a huge success with Russian audiences and still holds its place in the repertoires of theaters today.

In Verstovsky and Alyabyev's operas (they often wrote as a team), the vocal style of the Russian musical theater was formed. Verstovsky saw the basis for his new type of opera in the breadth and the warmth and the great depth of expression of song. Varlamov, an unrivalled specialist in singing who was for many years assistant conductor with the Bolshoi, was without doubt a great help to Verstovsky in the training of Russian opera singers. The fact that for a long time there had been no attempt to differentiate between operatic and dramatic artists on the Russian stage also made a significant mark on the new style of national singing and firmly established the actor-singer in the Russian theater, who was to enrapture audiences with his dramatic performance and create a musical illusion on stage. Outstanding among singers of the day were Bantyshev, a pure Russian, sweeping tenor with a broad range, Bulakhov, famous for his "velvet" voice, his depth of feeling for music and careful performance, and Lavrov, whom nature had generously endowed with great singing and acting talent. Perhaps the most gifted actor of all in the Petrovsky Theater was Repina, Verstovsky's wife. Apart from her technique and quality of performance onstage, which marked her out from the rest, she was an outstanding operatic singer and actress, and the first to perform many of the women's parts in Verstovsky's operas.

From the time of its birth in the feudal theater, the dramatic quality and expressive realism of the Moscow ballet set it apart from all others. In the years 1815 to 1825, the Russian ballet established itself in its own right, determined to achieve its most difficult aim, to found its own style of national classical dance.

At that time, Adam Glushkovsky, the outstanding and talented classical dancer and mime actor, who was also a ballet master and teacher, had started to work in Moscow. A pupil and follower of the famous Didelot, he brought his best fantastic-mythological and heroic-romantic ballets to the Moscow stage, and contributed much work on the new Russian repertoire. Without a doubt the most important event of all was Glushkovsky's production in 1821 of the ballet *Russlan and Ludmilla,* which was the first time that anyone had tried to choreograph any of Pushkin's works. During these years a wealth of national dances were adapted for the stage as an integral part of various ballets. The appearance of these in the midst of classical ballet could not help but influence it, and this led to the birth of the Russian school of classical dance, based on steps and arrangements used in national dancing, an achievement which is widely considered to be the greatest of that period. The precision, individuality, expressiveness, and realistic mimicry typical of Russian folk dancing were incorporated into the Russian ballet, making it unique.

The 1820s and 1830s were a period of great achievement for the Russian ballet. They saw the arrival of the romantic school. The Bolshoi produced Y. Sankovskaya, the first Russian ballerina to hold her own successfully among the best ballerinas in the world. Her popularity outstripped anything ever before known in the history of Russian dance. By combining her great talent with the realistic traditions of the Russian theater, she brought an entirely new approach to the first Moscow production of the romantic

ballet *Giselle,* produced by Taglioni. The realistic treatment of themes distinguished the Russian romantic ballet sharply from foreign schools.

At the same time work continued in Moscow to create national ballets. In 1830, Lobanov's popular divertissement *The Return of the Gallant Dons from War* was produced, and subsequently a new version of *Russlan and Ludmilla* by Glushkovsky appeared, and also his own version of the divertissement *The Beautiful Tatiana on Sparrow Hills.* The music for these was written by the leading Russian composers of the day, Alyabyev and Varlamov.

The Moscow ballet soon proved its ability to use the new language of dance to create exciting choreographic variations. It is interesting to note in this context that progressive Russian audiences of the time were very critical of foreign repertoires, and expected of them the same profoundly idealistic content and technique they found in their own Russian ballet. The actual content continued to be all-important in the Moscow ballet, while in the St. Petersburg ballet, form was the main concern. This explains why for nearly half a century the development of Russian ballet was centered on Moscow.

The year 1842 saw the commencement of a new era in the history of the Bolshoi Theater. On September 7 of that year, the very first Russian classic opera appeared on its stage, the new "national, tragic-heroic opera," *Ivan Susanin* by Glinka. Four years later, on December 9, 1846, Glinka's second opera, *Russlan and Ludmilla,* was heard for the first time. These dates have gone down in the history of the Bolshoi Theater, the pages of which have subsequently been filled with names such as Dargomizhsky, Serov, Tchaikovsky, Rubinstein, Rimsky-Korsakov, Borodin, Rachmaninov, and other great musicians who are the fathers of Russian music. Their work is intrinsically linked with that of the great Russian writers and poets—Pushkin, Lermontov, Gogol, Ostrovsky—whose subjects they had turned to for inspiration. Later, the theater's repertoire was further augmented by Serov's operas *Judith* and *Rogneda.*

It was largely due to the influence of Glinka's and Dargomizhsky's operas that the Bolshoi developed realism as its basic principle in opera.

The opera *Ivan Susanin* had a great influence not only on the development of Russian national opera but also on that of Russian national ballet. The ballet scenes in Glinka's operas were by no means considered to be of secondary importance, as backup numbers, as they were in works by foreign composers.

The dances in *Ivan Susanin,* and later on in *Russlan,* could not be removed without spoiling the piece as a whole. This completely different attitude towards dance within opera was to shape the original development of Russian national ballet for some time to come.

In March 1853 a huge fire in the Bolshoi completely wrecked its interior and most of the contents. Three years later the theater was completely rebuilt by an architect named Kavos. Thanks to him the acoustic and visual faults that the old Bolshoi had suffered from were eliminated in the new theater, and all that remained of the previous building were the outside walls and the colonnaded façade. The new Bolshoi, as it now stands, was opened on August 20, 1856 (according to the old calendar).

The Bolshoi Theater was becoming firmly established as a home for the treasure-house of Russian arts and national music, but it was a highly complicated and difficult process.

In the same year of 1842, the direction of the Moscow theaters was transferred to the Directorate of Imperial Theaters of St. Petersburg. The free hand in matters of repertoire and direction that the Moscow theater had enjoyed for the past decade—its originality and independence—was about to come face to face with the scornful attitude of the Emperor's clerks in St. Petersburg.

In the very years when the masterpieces of Russian classical opera were being written, Russian national art on the Moscow stage was forced into the position of pariah.

In 1861 the Directorate of Imperial Theaters handed the Bolshoi over to an Italian opera company, which performed there four or five days a week, leaving Russian opera with virtually only one day per week. Although it is true that competition between the two opera companies considerably helped the Russian singers, forcing them to constantly perfect their performances and to borrow a few hints from the Italian school, the scornful attitude of the Directorate towards the national repertoire and the privileged position given to foreign companies on tour made it very difficult for the Russian company to work and to win public recognition. Progressive forces within the theater struggled long and hard against the traditions of the court theater in favour of the originality and folk character of national ballet and opera.

The production of Tchaikovsky's opera *Eugene Onegin* in 1881 (which had only been produced once before by the Moscow Conservatory) can well be considered a turning point in the history of the Bolshoi. Its brilliant success heralded a great step forward in the life of the theater; from that time onwards, operas by Tchaikovsky and other Russian composers started to appear more frequently and with ever greater success on its stage. It was not long before the best of Tchaikovsky's works had all been performed—*Mazeppa* (1884), *Cherevichki (The Little Shoes,* 1887), *The Enchantress* (1870), *The Queen of Spades* (1891), *Iolanthe* (1893). In the same period, Rubinstein's *The Demon* (1875) and Serov's *The Power of Evil* (1871) also became part of the Bolshoi's repertoire.

The greatest victory of all for the Bolshoi was the appearance on its stage of operas by the Moguchaya Kuchka (the Great Group) composers, including Rimsky-Korsakov, Mussorgsky, Borodin, the masters of Russian classical opera. In 1888 Mussorgsky's opera *Boris Godunov* had its premiere, and in 1893 so did Rimsky-Korsakov's

The Snow Maiden, and in 1898 Borodin's *Prince Igor.* They were all met with wide acclaim and standing ovations from Russian high society, because they were unique in their wide scope and realism, in their true understanding of national character as expressed in the scenes showing the people, in which the music was based on folk melodies arranged to suit the inflections of ordinary Russian speech, thus giving them a dramatic significance greater than any works previously written. Yet even so, the stubborn resistance of the bureaucracy ensured that these masterpieces of Russian opera were always held up: only with great difficulty did they succeed in appearing on the imperial stage at all.

The basic principles of the Kuchka composers were the true expression of the lives of ordinary people as they really were and the sense of being one nation. The themes of their works are mostly taken from episodes in ordinary people's lives, Russia's past history, epic poems, and folktales.

By developing and enriching the traditions of Glinka and Dargomizhsky, these great musicians guided the Russian composers' school into a period of unprecedented success and achievement, and led it firmly onto the world stage.

In the second half of the nineteenth century, the Bolshoi company suddenly produced a whole galaxy of outstanding Russian singers, such as Semyonova (the first Muscovite singer to perform Antonida, Ludmilla, and Natasha), Aleksandrova-Kochetova, Lavrovskaya, Khokhlov (first to perform *Onegin* and *The Demon),* Korsov, Donskoi, Deisha-Sionitskaya, Salina, Preobrazhenskaya, and others.

The artistic demands made by the Russian classical repertoire forced the theater into improving the quality of its musical management and performance. In 1882 Altani became director-general of the Bolshoi Theater, and Avranek was appointed chorus leader. Tchaikovsky and Rubinstein directed their own operas. Greater attention was paid to set design and to the overall artistic preparation of productions than ever before.

Towards the end of the nineteenth century, the Bolshoi Ballet at last managed to overcome all obstacles and to emerge as a company in its own right, despite the bureaucrats' efforts to crush it. It had struggled for a long time against the influence of Western European theatrical tradition, and continued its search for new ways to develop its own choreographic style. In the second half of the nineteenth century, outstanding dancers such as Bogdanova, Lebedeva, Nikolayeva, Roslavleva and Geltzer, among others, were already regularly performing. Thanks to them a purely Russian style of choreography was developed, the fame of which spread far beyond the borders of Russia.

In 1877, the Bolshoi staged Tchaikovsky's first ballet, *Swan Lake.* The fact that this was the first ballet to be put on by the theater, that its content was astutely psychological and its music based on developing symphony music, made this ballet a landmark. It marked a basic change in the role of music in ballet. Suddenly ballet music, which in the popular ballets of the nineteenth-century composers Pugni and Minkus, had been of secondary importance, more a decoration than a piece of work in its own right, became an all important part of a visual production. Tchaikovsky gave to ballet the powerful realism and expression of his symphonic and operatic works. It was in his ballets that music, for the first time, made its debut as the language of feeling and passion.

Around the beginning of the twentieth century, the Bolshoi Theater entered its truly golden age, and became famous as one of the world's main music and ballet centers. The best operas in the world were to be found in its repertoire; operas by Mozart, Rossini, Verdi, Meyerbeer, Bizet, Wagner, Berlioz, Leoncavallo, Mascagni, Puccini. At the same time, however, Russian opera occupied the main place in its activity. One after the other, all of Rimsky-Korsakov's operas were produced: *The Maid of Pskov (Ivan the Terrible,* 1901), *The Governor or Pan Voyevoda* (1905), *Sadko* (1906), *The Legend of the Invisible City of Kitezh* (1908), *May Night* and *The Golden Cockerel* (1909). So were Dargomizhsky's operas *Russalka* (1900) and *The Stone Guest* (1906), Rachmaninov's *Aleko* (1893), *The Miserly Knight* and *Francesca da Rimini* (1906), and others.

At that time the Bolshoi Theater had a stronger company than ever before. Its orchestra, under the direction of Rachmaninov, Suk, and Cooper, was making a large contribution to the musical world in Moscow, and became the theater's pride and joy. The chorus, under Avranek's direction, reached its peak of perfection. Famous artists came to Moscow to design the settings, men such as

Above: A drawing showing the façade of the Grand Petrovsky Theater, completed in 1824 by Osip Ivanovich Bovet according to plans by A. Mikhailov.
On the following pages: The auditorium and stage of the Bolshoi Theater during a performance of Peter Tchaikovsky's Eugene Onegin.

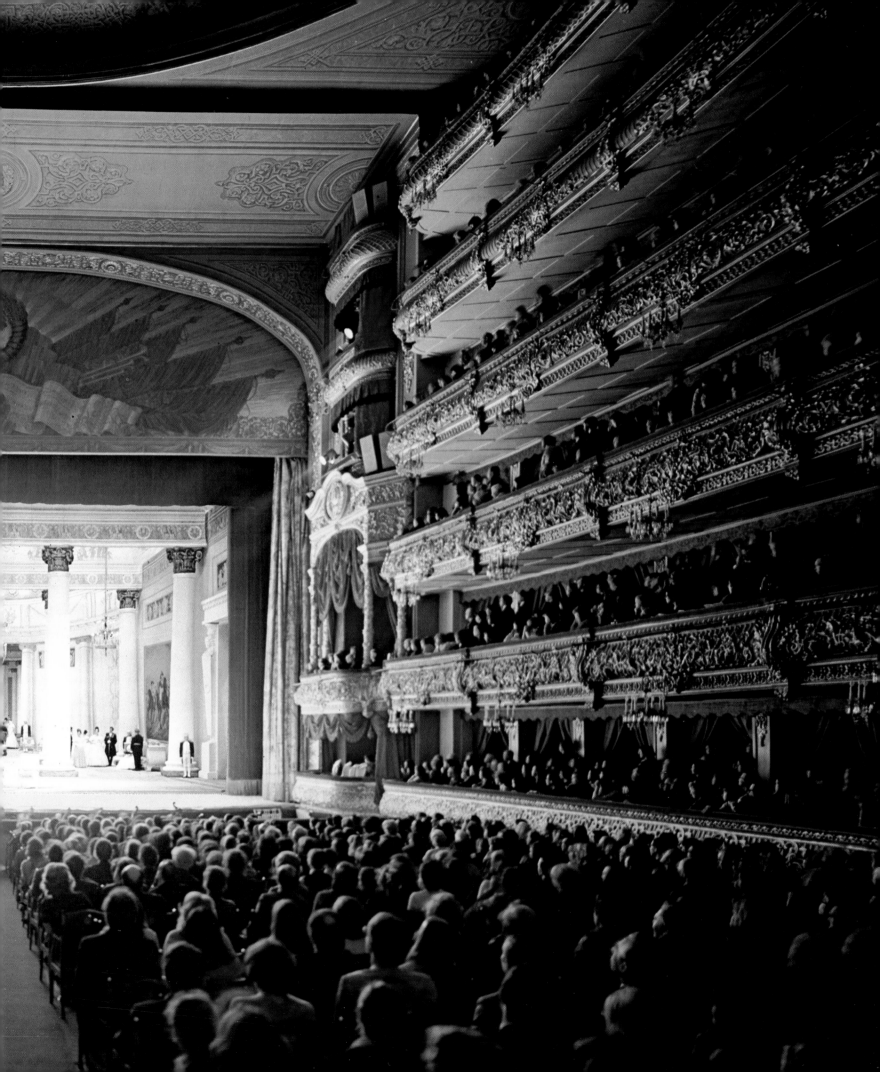

Vasnetsov, Golovin, and Korovin. The first steps towards the foundation of a directors' school were taken.

By the turn of the century, Russian singers had developed their own style based on the same principles as Russian music in general, namely purity and simplicity of performance, humanitarianism, and fidelity to the poetic message of the music and to that of the songs which always had their story to tell, while expressing genuine and soul-searching sentiments. The successes of the national choral school paved the way for the appearance in the Bolshoi of three great singers, Nezhdanova, Sobinov, and Chaliapin. A whole constellation of outstanding Russian singers worked together with them, such as Zruyeva, Stepanova, Alchevsky, Bogdanovich, Bonachich, Baklanov, Grizunov, Petrov, Smirnov, Pirogov, and Savransky.

The leading figures in the Bolshoi Opera consolidated the traditions of realistic interpretation of roles in Russian opera, the search for the inner meaning, simplicity, and purity of works, while at the same time maintaining high quality of choral performance—traditions which still hold good today.

These characteristics of Russian theatrical style were best embodied in the works of Chaliapin, that great genius who more or less became the living personification of the creative will. Chaliapin was a people's artist, as great a singer as he was an actor, and it was he who raised Russian musical and dramatic art to their zenith. His activity was to mark a major stage in the history of world opera. The characters he brought to life—Susanin, Melnik, Holofernes, Boris Godunov, Ivan the Terrible, Salieri, Galitsky, Mephistopheles, Philip II, and others—are examples of perfection reached by a great master deeply committed to realism. They will probably never be equalled.

The beginning of the twentieth century saw the opening of a period of flourishing development for the Bolshoi Ballet. The fact that ballet, as it were, followed in opera's footsteps by turning to Russian classical music, contributed to its rise at this time. One after the other, three of the greatest Russian classical ballets entered its repertoire, the *Sleeping Beauty, Raymonda,* and *Swan Lake.* Since then, these great classics have become an integral and much loved part of the Ballet's repertoire. The Bolshoi's ballet master of the time, Gorsky, set about reforming the ideas of the company, which, until then, had adhered to the idea of artistic unity within every production, synthesizing dance, drama, music and design. Ballets which he produced—such as *Don Quixote,* to music by Minkus (1901), *The Humpbacked Horse or the Tsar-Maiden* by Pugni (1901), *Vain Precautions* to music by Hertel (1903), *Coppelia* to Delibes's music, and many others—occupy a proud place in the history of Russian ballet. During the same period such talented dancers as Geltzer, Mordkin, and Tikhomirov were receiving world acclaim.

The great achievements of the Russian ballet and opera at the beginning of the twentieth century could not, however, mask the difficulties which beset the development of their art within the imperial theater. Far-reaching reforms were needed, which could not hope to take place within a regime such as the one then existing.

The October Revolution turned a new page in world history. It affected every area of life in Russia, including, of course, the theater. The theater, which had previously been a closed institution or a private one, catering to the tastes of a small elite, suddenly turned into a cultural force to be reckoned with, an institution for the people.

From the very earliest days of Soviet power, the Bolshoi, together with other large theaters, became subject to the jurisdiction of the People's Commission for Enlightenment, with the aim of trying to satisfy working people's desire for art and culture. The Bolshoi company gradually built up a close and indissoluble relationship with the people through its broad-based audiences, starting with concert-meetings at which its members actually met soldiers and commanders of the Red Army, workers, and peasants. The company was very aware of and greatly valued the people's

Above: The fire which in March 1853 gutted the Grand Petrovsky Theater (drawing by E. Lile). Only the external walls and the columns of the façade remained of the old building.
On the following pages: Two details of the Bolshoi Theater, the curtain and the auditorium during an intermission.

thirst for art and culture, and tried to meet this need by opening wide its doors to the masses.

In its first Soviet season, the Bolshoi Theater produced 170 operas and ballets.

Apart from productions onstage, shows were organized in other venues, such as workers' clubs, railway clubs, military units, not only in Moscow, but also in the area surrounding it, and all the company's leading performers took part in them.

In the 1918–19 season, the Bolshoi orchestra started giving symphony concerts in which leading musicians such as Nezhdanova, Sobinov, Petrov, and others took part. A group of soloists from the opera, under the young conductor Golovanov, staged many Russian and Western operas in various clubhouses.

During the difficult years of the civil war, the theater was faced with the worrying problem of how to protect its artistic and material values, to preserve the theater as an integral whole, and its tradition of staging the best works produced by Russian composers, including the masterpieces of such talented set designers as Vasnetsov, Golovin, and Korovin. But preserving the past for posterity was not the only important task. The theater's activity as a whole had to be rethought, bureaucratic methods of management replaced, the repertoire enlarged, new forms sought. The theater had to be brought within the reach of the masses, who had previously never been able to go to ballets and operas. All these problems had to be resolved under economically difficult conditions, when sufficient financial means were not to be found. True to the words of Lenin, that every effort must be made to ensure that "the main pillars of our culture do not fall," the Communist Party and Soviet government managed, even in those difficult times, to find the means to help the Bolshoi Theater in every possible way. This policy ran up against bitter opposition from members of the Organization for Culture and Education under the People's Commission for Enlightenment, and also from "leftists" who had sworn to obliterate all traces of art from the past. Thanks to Lenin's intervention, however, the Bolshoi Theater was saved.

During this period, the first People's Commissar for Enlightenment, Anatoly V. Lunacharsky, also did much for the Bolshoi.

In 1919, the Bolshoi was honoured by the title "Academic," and in 1924, an offshoot was opened in the buildings of the former Zimina private opera house. Shows were produced there right up until 1959.

The sociocultural role which the Bolshoi had to fulfill in the Soviet era led to an immeasurable increase in the company's activity. Leading artists in the theater such as Sobinov, Nezhdanova, Geltzer, Derzhinskaya, Obukhova, Katulskaya, Stepanova, Petrov, Pirogov, Migai, Savransky, Gorsky, Krieger, Tikhomirov, and others who had made their debut even before the Revolution, continued to perform before their new audiences.

Many Russian classics were renovated or produced for the first time, including a large number that had never before been performed in their entirety in public owing to censorship. The staging of *Boris Godunov* in 1927 was a red-letter day as it was the first full-length production of the work, including the previously censored scenes in the Kromy Forest and outside St. Basil's. In 1925, Mussorgsky's opera Sorochinsky Fair was premiered, and perhaps an even greater moment was Gorodetsky's readaptation of *Ivan Susanin.* At the same time a great deal of effort was being put into the production of foreign classics by composers such as Wagner, Mozart, Verdi, and Puccini.

The ballet repertoire was not being ignored, either. In 1919 the first performance of Tchaikovsky's *Nutcracker* took place in Moscow, and in 1921 Stravinsky's *Petrushka. Swan Lake, The Sleeping Beauty, Raymonda, Giselle, Don Quixote,* to mention but a few, were brought back to the Moscow stage in new adaptations. To complement these, there were also many ballets being produced to music that was not written for the theater at all.

The Bolshoi, however, found itself faced with the task of creating a new repertoire. Soviet librettists were finding it very difficult to adapt to the new contemporary opera and ballet, but the Bolshoi was not going to give up. Despite frequent mistakes and failures, the Bolshoi gradually moved towards its goal. In 1924 the very first opera with music by a Soviet composer was produced on the stage of the Bolshoi—Yurovsky's *Trilby.* Hard on its heels followed Vasilenko's ballet *Joseph the Beautiful* and operas by Triodin, Stephan Razin and Zolotarev *(The Decembrists).* In 1927 the theater produced for the first time one of Prokofiev's works, his opera *The Love of the Three Oranges.* Finally, in the same year, to mark the tenth anniversary of the October Revolution, the Bolshoi Theater staged *The Red Poppy,* a ballet which is considered to be one of the foundation stones of Soviet dance, being the first fully fledged expression of the new contemporary Soviet musical and choreographic art. Soon the first, comparatively naive, attempts at opera on contemporary themes appeared, such as Pototsky's *The Breakthrough* and Korchmarev's *Ivan the Soldier.* In the thirties, the Bolshoi company gained much useful experience and know-how in its work on production of Dzerzhinsky's two operas, *The Quiet Don* and *Virgin Soil Upturned,* and Chishko's *Battleship Potemkin.* In 1935 they produced Shostakovich's opera *Lady Macbeth of Mtsensk.* The thirties also saw the appearance of such ballets as Asafiev's *The Flames of Paris,* and *Fountain of Bakhchisarai,* which were to become classics of the Soviet ballet repertoire.

Each year brought new premieres, the search for something different, all of which continuously enriched the company's fund of experience.

During the Second World War, which rudely interrupted the peaceful, creative work of the Bolshoi Theater, the company still

managed to fulfill its civil duty with honour. Both those members of it evacuated to Kuibyshev and the many who remained behind in Moscow continued with their work. Faithful to its fundamental principles of creativity even during the stormy years of the war, the Bolshoi Theater did not cease to work on new productions, producing Kabalevsky's opera *In the Fire* and Yurovsky's ballet *Crimson Sails;* as it stood proud and erect, a symbol of peace and beauty in the motherland, it was a source of inspiration to the people in their fight against fascism.

In the years following the war, the Bolshoi turned more to operas written by composers from socialist countries. Produced for the first time on stage of the Bolshoi and its offshoot were *The Bartered Bride* by Smetana, *Halka* by Moniuszko, *Fidelio* by Beethoven, *Bánk Bán* by Erkel, *Jenůfa* by Janáček, and *Duke Bluebeard's Castle* by Bartók.

Its productions of *Boris Godunov, Khovanshchina, Sadko,* and *Prince Igor* were notable for their depth of feeling and their musical and dramatic purity—so much so that they run unaltered even today. Prokofiev's ballets *Romeo and Juliet* and *Cinderella* became lasting examples of Soviet classical ballet at its best.

In the fifties and sixties, the theater once again started to enlarge its Soviet repertoire and also included new operas and ballets based on themes from world literature, such as Prokofiev's *War and Peace* taken from Tolstoy, Shebalin's *Taming of the Shrew* and Prokofiev's *Romeo and Juliet* taken from Shakespeare, Vasilenko's *Mirandolina* from Goldoni, Krein's *Laurencia* from Lope de Vega, *The Bronze Horseman* by Gliere from Pushkin, Shchedrin's *Dead Souls* from Gogol, to mention but a few. Whenever possible the theater produced operas and ballets based on Soviet literature. Examples of these are Kabalevsky's *Nikita Vershinin,* Khrennikov's *The Mother,* Prokofiev's *The Story of a Real Man,* Dzerzhinsky's *Man's Fate,* Kholminov's *Optimistic Tragedy,* Prokofiev's *Semyon Kotko* and Molchanov's *Here the Dawn Is Quiet;* notable among the ballets are Vlasov's *Asel* and Eshpaya's *Angara.* In these productions the hero of today has found his place in ballet and opera.

The premieres of new productions on completely original themes were milestones in the musical and theatrical life of the country. There were operas such as Shaporin's *The Decembrists* and Muradelli's *October,* ballets such as Khachaturian's *Spartacus,* Prokofiev's *Ivan the Terrible,* and Slonimsky's *Icarus.* The achievements of the Bolshoi Theater and Soviet composers in creating a new dramatic art, a new language of song, and new forms rich in content have had a far-reaching significance for Soviet art as a whole.

One of the worthiest of the Bolshoi's traditions is that of welcoming works by composers from the national republics. At various times works such as *Abessalom and Eteri* by Paliashvili, *Almast* by Spendiarov, *Song of the Woods* by Zhukovsky, *Gayane* by Khachaturian, *Leili and Medzhun* by Balasanian, *Shurale* by Yarullina, *Dzhaliel* by Zhiganov, *Path of Thunder* by Karayev, *Leg-*

end of Love by Melikov, and, finally, one of the most recent premieres in the theater, *Abduction of the Moon* by Taktakishvili. These productions, all of them fine examples of the wealth of culture to be found within the multinational Soviet Union, have made a truly great contribution to its overall cultural environment and development, and have helped to consolidate the friendship existing between the nations which make up this great country.

In the Soviet era the role of the director has increased considerably in the search for a true understanding of authors' works and their interpretation. He is also largely responsible for rehearsing and preparing actors who will be capable of creating psychologically true, "living" characters who are not merely empty shells. Likewise, the whole company nowadays has a larger say in the artistic and ideological problems which occur, and these are solved thanks to the professionalism of the orchestra, chorus, and other members of the theater. All of these factors, taken together, have created the "Bolshoi style" and brought the theater worldwide fame.

From its earliest days since the Revolution, the Bolshoi Theater has made every effort to improve the standard of the visual backup work that goes into every production. In 1918 the Stanislavsky opera studio was formed within the theater; this studio was mainly responsible for the subsequent development of Soviet musical and theatrical artistic design. Gradually the Soviet school of producers started to take shape in the persons of Lossky, Smolich, and Baratov.

Through the work of talented designers such as Fyedorovsky, Dmitriyev, Williams, and later Ryndin, the Bolshoi's own style of set design was developed. It is essentially realistic, and is conceived on a monumental scale tailored especially to the requirements of the Bolshoi's stage and the productions that take place on it.

We must not omit to mention at this juncture the achievements of the chorus, which was going from strength to strength under the leadership of Avranek and Shorin.

The extraordinary talents of the great Galina Ulanova were also fostered and developed on the Bolshoi's stage.

The Soviet school of choreography was likewise gradually establishing itself. Its leading exponents, Lavrovsky, Zakharov, Vainonen, and Goleizovsky, choreographed many outstanding ballets which have gone into the annals of Soviet classical ballet.

The Bolshoi Theater has an immeasurable influence on the spiritual, moral, and ideological education of Soviet people. Its art opens up to people the music of the world around them, points the way to the high ideals of harmonious perfection, of spirituality and morality of the purest kind, shows life in its most festive yet heroic moments, with all its poetry and beauty. At the same time it is supremely democratic and correct in both form and content. The principles of realism and democracy, bequeathed to it by the founders of Russian music and theatre, have been and still are being developed in the work of the Bolshoi's outstanding masters. In the years of Soviet power, the Bolshoi Theater has nurtured several generations of brilliant artists in both opera and ballet.

There are at the present time many notable singers in the Bolshoi Opera company. The names of Obraztsova, Arkhipova, Milashkina, Atlantov, Mazurok, Nesterenko, Eisen, Sotkilava, Pyavko, Malennikov, Ognivtsev, Vedernikov, Rudenko, and Gulyayev are well known to opera fans in many countries of the world.

Much of the credit for the development of contemporary opera belongs to Pokrovsky, who for many years was the principal director with the Bolshoi Theater. His work is characterized by a careful attention to the author's text, by an intelligent and sensitive read-

ing of the musical drama of works, by a special feeling for culture, and by his professionalism.

The Bolshoi Ballet enjoys unfading glory. The names of a whole constellation of famous ballet dancers decorate the present-day Bolshoi Ballet company, names such as Plisetskaya, Bessmertnova, Maximova, Struchkova, Timofeyeva, Kondratyeva, Sorokina, Semenyanka, Pavlova, Vasiliev, Lavrovsky, Liepa, Vladimirov, Godunov, Akimov, Gordeyev, and many others.

For many years now the principal ballet director with the Bolshoi has been Yuri Grigorovich. His work constitutes a major stage in the development of Soviet ballet. Ballets directed by him stand out owing to the maximum dramatic expression he manages to put into dance, his exhaustive exploration of the choreographic possibilities, and his extensive use of imagery. The ballet *Spartacus* to music by Khachaturian is perhaps the supreme example of Grigorovich's style. This ballet is generally considered to be the greatest achievement in Soviet ballet in recent times.

The Bolshoi Theater orchestra is renowned the world over. Its principal director Simonov, and conductors Khaikin, Lazarev, Ermler, Mansurov, Zhuraitis, and Kopylov, continue to expand through their work the great tradition of the Bolshoi Theater conductors' school—traditions laid down by Golovanov, Pasovsky, Melik-Pashayev, Samosud, and Faier, and later continued by Svetlanov, Kondrashin, and Rozhdestvensky. Under the direction of the principal choirmaster, Rybnov, and his assistants Agafonnikov, Khazanov, Gusev, and Lykov, the Bolshoi Theater chorus has made enormous progress. The artistic legacy of the Bolshoi Theater is continued and expanded by the principal set designer Zolotarev and his assistant Leventhal.

In the years of Soviet power, the creative process in the Bolshoi Theater has taken on a new character, becoming the center of Soviet multinational art. Under the Bolshoi's guidance, drawing on its experience and achievements in the arts, opera and ballet companies have been formed in republics which had not even heard of this type of theater before the Revolution.

More than one generation has been brought up on the art of the Bolshoi in the U.S.S.R. The Bolshoi Theater is a living witness to history, a wise preserver of classical art, a symbol of the continuity of generations of leading Russian artists, the embodiment of life's continuity. But at the same time the Bolshoi Theater is intricately linked to life, life which surrounds the theater, fills it and enriches it. Its links with the people are indissoluble because it was the people who founded the Bolshoi and who determined its fate.

Members of the Bolshoi Theater company regularly go away to take part in the construction of power stations, new roads, and railways. There is a fine tradition of going on tour each year to build up an artistic rapport between the Bolshoi Theater and the various regions of the Soviet Union.

The influence of the Bolshoi Theater in the world arena is like-

Top: The Bolshoi Theater after the reconstruction of 1856 to plans by A. K. Kavos (drawing by V. Sadovnikov). It was opened on August 20 according to the old calendar.
Bottom: The foyer of the theater after the reconstruction, shown in an engraving made in 1861.

wise great. Its masters contribute much to the production of operas and ballets in many countries. Its foreign tours have had exceptional influence on international music and have established the company as one of the best in its field, making it possible for the world to see with its own eyes the brilliant successes and achievements in Soviet arts.

The Communist Party and Soviet government greatly esteem the Bolshoi Theater. It has twice (in 1937 and 1976) been awarded the Lenin Prize. About seventy of its members have received the title of People's Artists of the U.S.S.R., seven are Lenin Prize winners themselves, and Galina Ulanova has been honoured with the title of Hero of Socialist Labour.

Leonid Brezhnev has called the Bolshoi Theater "the academy of national musical culture." The company has always striven and will always strive to justify the great faith shown in it.

Alexander Ivanovich Gusov

Opposite: The façade of the Bolshoi Theater. After the Revolution of October 1917, the theater was restructured and reopened to the public on April 8, 1918, with an act from Russlan and Ludmilla *by Mikhail Glinka and an act from* Sadko *by Nikolai Rimsky-Korsakov.*

THE LYRIC OPERA

The repertoire of the Bolshoi Theater is based on three fundamental elements of inspiration: Russian musical tradition, the spreading of Western drama, and exploring life as it really is.

A Glorious Path

The history of our theater began the day a small troupe was formed, the consistent activity of which not even fires, changes of government, changes of management, or official court policy could disrupt.

It is interesting that from the very beginning this theater developed and grew as the embodiment of the Russian national realistic tradition; it is also interesting that the Bolshoi, born out of the spiritual needs of the progressive and democratic echelons of society in the second half of the eighteenth century, has maintained and is still building upon its original artistic and social principles. National character, realism, and democracy were always the colours on the flag of its art. Throughout its existence these colours have guided it to success in its work; to forget them would lead to inevitable downfall. Neither temporary distractions, the pursuit of fashion, nor the cries of pseudo innovators could rock these traditions. For it was these very same traditions which were the driving force behind the growth of Russian operatic art, these very same traditions which prevented it from falling into the trap of mediocrity.

Tradition always supposes development and movement. Tradition and innovation are not contradictions, but rather two sides of the one coin. Tradition, without the quest for what is new, becomes routine. When considering the ideological and artistic traditions of the Bolshoi Theater, a whole series of names comes to mind, names of writers and performers who are famous for being innovators in their own particular field. Among the composers are Glinka, Mussorgsky, Borodin, Tchaikovsky, Rimsky-Korsakov, and Rachmaninov; among the singers, Chaliapin, Sobinov, Nezhdanova, Khokhlov, and Zbruyeva; then there is Korovin, the great set designer, and there are others from the cream of the Bolshoi who preserve its glorious tradition.

Many others have been forgotten as mediocre stereotypes. It may be that they were very professional in their work and were locally very successful, yet they did not leave their mark on the development of Russian art. The history of the Bolshoi Theater teaches us not only to preserve but—just as important—to develop traditions, as the following examples will show.

Tchaikovsky's *Eugene Onegin,* produced in the Bolshoi Theater in 1881, was in every respect an avant-garde production. This opera shocked many reactionaries and provoked biting criticism from "experts" and mockery from those devoid of any foresight whatsoever and incapable of understanding what was happening around them. The novelty of Tchaikovsky lay in his ability to remain true to life and to create psychologically complex characters with human sentiments, and in his disregard for operatic and theatrical devices. This was not just another novelty, it was a bold statement of the national, realistic principles of Russian opera. This was one of those happy examples of the portrayal of contemporary life on the Bolshoi's stage. Yet how many people, even friends, tried to persuade the composer to abandon this "theme, unsuitable for the stage"?

Every great operatic production brings forth its great performers. And, naturally, we associate the fame of two prominent members of the Bolshoi company, Khokhlov and Sobinov, with *Eugene Onegin*. Is it possible, for instance, to talk about Chaliapin and not associate his innovative genius with the works of Mussorgsky?

Boris Godunov was not produced in the Bolshoi Theater until 1881, fully sixteen years after Mussorgsky wrote it! The "legislators of good taste" would not accept for a long time the ideological content of the opera, its profound psychology and folk roots. Neither did they like the composer's musical style, his refusal to round off arias and cantatas with sweet little melodies to soothe their satiated ears.

Boris Godunov was an avant-garde work developing the trend of Russian art based on folk drama. Subsequently, Mussorgsky described his *Khovanshchina* as a folk musical drama. This marked the opening of new social and artistic horizons in operatic art.

In 1896, with the aim of making the opera more successful, Rimsky-Korsakov reedited and reorchestrated *Boris Godunov*. To a certain extent he simply adapted the awkward passages in Mussorgksy's original score to suit the taste and requirements of the Imperial Theater Directorate, ruler of destinies in the art world at that time. However, Rimsky-Korsakov, with the frankness of a truly great artist, admitted that this was only to be considered as a temporary alteration, and that Mussorgsky's score would eventually come back into its own.

If we were to make a list of Chaliapin's masterpieces, then his performance in the role of Boris Godunov would surely be the first to spring to mind. There is much to be learned from the profound understanding that this great man had of Mussorgsky's music; how he recognized its folk spirit and minutely understood the composer's intentions. He had his own unique style of rendition in recitative and managed to penetrate the very essence of the work so well that it soon became impossible to separate the original piece from the finished performance. The true spirit of the people, the inner depths of man's trials and tribulations, the unique quality of national characteristics, are all put into one melting pot and the characters that emerge from it have always been and always will be the ideal guiding the genuine artist in the world of opera.

It would not be possible to imagine the present repertoire of the Bolshoi Theater without Borodin's opera *Prince Igor*. Yet it took a great deal of time and persistent demands from the more democratic elements of the public and even petitions with many hundreds of signatures before it was allowed to be produced on the Moscow stage. It was not until 1898 that *Prince Igor* first appeared at the Bolshoi Theater. Borodin's original idea was in itself a great leap forward in the Russian arts; he wanted to develop Glinka's principles further, and in so doing founded the epic production, uniting patriotism with history and the psychology of the individual.

Lyrical scenes, folk music, drama, and epic poems—all of them completely different genres, different artistically, esthetically—yet how much they all have in common within the school of Russian opera, with its ideological, realistic, and popular nature!

It seems strange to us nowadays to read about the difficulties that were encountered in trying to create the repertoire that has become the foundation stone of the Bolshoi Theater, and the banner of its traditions. However, even in difficulties there is a certain kind of logic. A great artist will foresee the development of art and will concentrate on his own creativity, disregarding what may be popular and widespread, and will rather nurture the first buds of future development. The contemporary genius will perceive progressive tendencies, sorting out what is really valuable from among them, and will not confine his activity within the bounds of what is already established and known to all. This is the artist who will help social progress and who will be the driving force behind art and the development of its traditions.

This process has not been an easy one in the Bolshoi Theater. This was not solely due to the mediocrity of taste among certain members of the audience, but to a well-defined programme dictated by the autocracy, a programme aimed at separating art from the country's stormy social development and reducing it to a harmless pleasure unlikely to provoke thought about anything in particular. Thus the theater was ablaze with the luxuriant costumes of demigods and half-human creatures, grandiose sets with fireworks and magical transformations all crowned with the transient glory of performing stars standing temporarily in the limelight. It was not just a question of taste, it was a manifestation of reaction in art.

It is significant that the realistic principles developing at that time in the Bolshoi Theater were also making themselves apparent in productions of works by Western composers. An example of this is Leonid Sobinov's interpretation of Wagner's *Lohengrin*. This terrible Knight of the Grail, fighting with the sword for the honour of the sacred title, became a living man in the Russian's interpretation of the character, noble and compassionate towards the victims of injustice and vice. The radiant figure of Sobinov as Lohengrin was the embodiment of the desire to achieve harmony of spirit and the victory of peace over force. It was not fear but suffering that was the essence of Sobinov's Lohengrin.

This was by no means the only example of such artistic transformation. We have only to consider Chaliapin's roles (Mephistopheles, King Philip, Basilio), or Nezhdanova's (Elsa, Violetta, Gilda).

Since then the Bolshoi's policy on repertoire has been based on three traditional types: Russian classical opera, Western European classical opera, and contemporary opera.

When in 1917 the Bolshoi Theater cast off the fetters of the Imperial Theater Directorate, it found itself facing new conditions, new demands and problems. The best of its prerevolutionary work now had to serve the new society. In such stormy times, uncertainty could well have crept into the world of art, which found itself in a wholly unfamiliar environment. It became the object of many bitter attacks by the advocates of the "new" direction. At this juncture it is impossible not to recall with deep gratitude how, even in the most difficult times for the young republic, Lenin uncompromisingly supported the great artistic achievements of the past, and in so doing protected the Bolshoi Theater, and saved it from closure.

In the new political atmosphere, the traditions of progressive, national realistic art were given complete freedom to develop and immediately became established as the theater's official policy on artistic activity.

This affected repertoire, performance, production. However, the most important change was that the new era endowed the theater with a new artistic school—the school of socialist realism.

Obviously, the new type of audience coming to the theater in 1917 had a decisive impact upon it.

The new problems and aims dictated by the new way of life naturally laid down a new code of conduct in the artistic organization of the theater. Even in the middle of the nineteenth century, the theatergoer could only with difficulty find the name of the director on his programme. Rachmaninov altered this by putting the director's name at the top of the cast list. Thanks to this, nowadays we can easily list the names of our theater's leading directors: Šuk, Golovanov, Pazovsky, Samosud, and Melik-Pashayev.

Set designers also began receiving the recognition due to them; artists such as Vasnetsov and Golovin, who were then working in the theater, consolidated the principles later to be taken up and developed by Fyedorovsky, Dmitriyev, Williams, Ryndin, and other outstanding Soviet designers.

But the arts of song and drama, as is the case with music and design, are only elements of a future synthesis. To produce an opera meeting contemporary requirements necessitates the unification of these elements into one whole. To produce an opera, which is a synthetic form, requires the organization of all the art forms which comprise it into the plan of one artist who has a clear conception of what the final result will be. This will not merely result in a bringing together of art forms but will ensure that they complement each other and work together as a whole. The ideological problems of each production, its creative organization, and the direction it should take are all areas requiring the expertise of the director. It was no accident that immediately following the October Revolution the Bolshoi Theater turned for help to Stanislavsky and Nemirovich-Danchenko. It is also no accident that the theater's new successes were linked with the names of such directors as Lossky, Smolich, Lapitsky, and Baratov.

The art of the director received not only the right to exist but also unprecedented responsibility—this last being a direct result of the new dimensions added to the Bolshoi Theater's traditions by the new ideology and school of socialist realism.

The Bolshoi Theater has existed for more than sixty years in the new society. It has become the recognized center of music and drama in our country. In 1922 it was designated the Bolshoi Theater of the Soviet Union. For the theater this does not merely represent an honour, to bear an illustrious title in recognition of its merits; great titles demand great deeds, and therefore it must continue to produce only work of the highest caliber. In the fast-moving, turbulent life of today, the history of the people, the continuous development of social and personal conditions and circumstances are the only guide to the development of artistic traditions and the absolute conditions of their existence.

We remember with gratitude those people who placed the art of the Bolshoi on a level worthy of the social and artistic requirements of our times. But we cannot forget that with each opera it stages a theater will adapt its artistic approach in line with current ideas and tastes.

A theater's artistic criteria are defined by changes in social requirements at any given time, although always within the established framework of its general principles.

The Bolshoi is a theater of tradition. This is far from being a reproach or a judgment. On the contrary, in this lies the theater's strength, its continued lease of life. But we must not confuse tradition with routine. Therefore the solutions found by famous directors in the past could seem to us today (and in fact sometimes do), to be naive and unconvincing. We have the right to—and in fact we should—consider with a critical eye the interpretations of classic productions which have appeared over the years in the Bolshoi. We should consider them in the hope that they will fire our imagination and help us to reach a better understanding of them by discovering in their scores and production notes new possibilities which we could expand upon today.

Glinka's opera *Russlan and Ludmilla* made its first appearance on stage as a cumbersome and slow-moving piece. In an attempt to overcome the resultant boredom, the conductors (directors at that time did not yet have enough authority), abridged the score, disregarding more often than not the main points of the dramatic composition and retaining only those numbers which conveyed the results of events and the action in general. The opera was turned into a collection of nice arias and melodies and lost its original identity.

Since then, however, the theater has realized the importance of the dramatic composition of operas and has done its best to make up for past error by reinstating previously discarded and forgotten pages. Thanks to this policy, it has found a new lease of life. Modern theatrical techniques help to explore thoroughly each opera and to interpret it as the composer himself had intended.

The modern-day director must also understand that if when producing an opera he disregards the author's original conception of it, and imposes only his own interpretation, then the final work produced will invariably be awkward and inartistic. With every new opera he directs, the modern director virtually has to step into a whole new world of art forms, and try to bring to life as faithfully as possible the esthetic and ethical ideas contained in it. The ideas of each great opera writer are unique and individual.

Opera is basically the relationship between a visual scene onstage and expression through music. In this relationship, both elements undergo a transformation and a new art is born—the art of the opera.

Alas, there still exists a tendency to divide opera into its component parts of music and theater. The hegemony of one and the obliteration of the other have caused the Bolshoi Theater many a headache and setback. That terrible enemy of the art, the destruction of the synthesis of opera, has been known to bring it very nearly to ruin. The unique quality of opera can only be born in the relationship between a dramatic scene onstage and the musical expression of it. The composer who is writing an opera sees all the while in his mind's eye the stage of a theater, and writes his work accordingly; he is not writing music to just sit back and listen to. The visual scene onstage should not become a mere illustration of the story told by the music, but must be a form born of the dramatic content of the music and, working together with it, must carve out the truth of genuine operatic art.

All of the Bolshoi's recent, contemporary operas are products of these principles. Such principles are not only important in modern opera, but must also govern the production of classics. It is from them that opera derives its unity, a unity that is achieved through the artistic cooperation of director and conductor, of artist and singer. This is why the participation of any, even the most talented, guest artist in the Bolshoi's best opera productions, destroys the unity which is so vital to the quality of the production.

Naturally there are still old-fashioned productions in existence which have survived until this day and have become identified with certain performers and companies. This highlights the constant spirit of change and renewal typical of the Bolshoi's work; it is constantly developing and adapting its ideas within the framework of its traditions, which are based on democracy; realism and adherence to the national character of the art.

Due to its many years of highly principled activity in the world of opera, the Bolshoi Theater naturally has great influence on the overall development of musical drama in our country, and also on the work of contemporary composers.

To a large extent, the taste of operagoers is defined by the theater itself. We always pay close attention to changes in the character of this influence and to the formation of contemporary taste in opera.

It must not be forgotten that the very fact that the Bolshoi came into existence created the possibility and necessity of this influence, as the theater itself was born as a result of the requirements of the time, and of the principles of democratic art. The theater was born as a collective enterprise, in the management of which the various echelons of the cultural intelligentsia would collaborate. It was under the direction of the theater council, made up of representatives of the literary world, musicians, teachers, historians, philosophers—all of them united by the same national and democratic ideals. The Bolshoi Theater (at that time it was not yet known under this name, and gave performances in many different venues) was not only an opera and ballet theater but also a drama theater.

During the ensuing period of consolidation in the arts and humanities, a center of learning grew up at this theater, which was to influence the development of art. Operas, ballets, plays, and short pieces taken from everyday life were being written for it. Other theaters, especially those in the provinces, looked to the repertoire of this theater for material. This art was in direct contrast to the pompous, aristocratic shows of the court theaters in St. Petersburg. The Moscow theater's tradition became so much a part of it that even many years under the thumb of the imperial court could not dissolve it.

It is only natural that in the Soviet era, when the Bolshoi Theater became the main "academy of national musical culture," its principles should have more influence than ever before.

A great number of artists, directors, and conductors from all the Union Republics spend a certain period of time in the theater in order to be able to work with and learn from it. Members of the Bolshoi Theater regularly go on tour to other theaters within the Soviet Union; these tours to all corners of our huge country have become one of the Bolshoi's traditions. The company has been to Kiev and Minsk, Leningrad and Yerevan, Tbilisi, Baku, Sverdlovsk, Novosibirsk, Volgograd, and other cities. During these tours they do not confine themselves to stage appearances, although it is precisely these which have such influence on the development of opera in the country. They take part in discussions and meetings of various kinds (for example, they go to workers' clubs, collective farms, military units, new towns, etc.) and spread information about the art of the Bolshoi Theater. The theater's authority has become so great that its own brand of opera production is sometimes used as a standard to copy from, which, sadly, can lead to stereotyping. Fortunately, the many different kinds of production the theater uses in succession prevent the formation of a stereotype which could be extremely detrimental to the art.

Perhaps it should be admitted that the Bolshoi's greatest influence, and the one which carries the greatest responsibility, is that over composers writing operas. The different aspects of our classical legacy evoke different reactions from the authors of operas on questions of style and form. The spiritual intimacy of Dzerzhinsky's operas, their clarity (and according to many, their somewhat primitive quality), exists side by side with the lyrical pathos of Molchanov, while the contemporary recitative, modulated language of Shchedrin is different from the national melodies of the Georgian composer Taktakishvili.

Of course, when writing a piece to be produced in the Bolshoi Theater, each composer bears in mind the conditions and possibilities of the theater—its stage, auditorium, type of audience, the abilities of the orchestra, chorus, and soloists, and the decor and props available—which means, in effect, that works adapted for the Bolshoi Theater, even before being presented, already echo its style and artistic principles. Working closely with different composers helps the company to progress by adding new colours to its creative palette and opening up new avenues of expression.

From this we can understand the great extent to which the Bolshoi Theater influences operatic art as a whole in our country.

We must add here that the official name of our theater is the Bolshoi Theater of the U.S.S.R. This name defines its creative work and accordingly imposes certain duties. While its company members constantly participate in the artistic life of many theaters in our multinational state, composers, artists, conductors, and directors from the Union and the autonomous republics are given access to and the right to air their own talents on the "main stage of the country."

In recent years the Bolshoi Theater company has started to make regular trips abroad; it has been to Berlin, New York, Milan, Warsaw, Prague, Vienna, Tokyo, Montreal, and Paris. Its productions on tour have always been a statement of its unchanged belief in realism and the indissoluble bond between art and the culture of the nation which engendered it.

The flowering of operatic art owes much to the great achievements of its exponents. If in this book you find long lists of well-known names connected with the Bolshoi of today, and if the roles that are attributed to them give you the impression of originality on the one hand and of the wealth and variation of the Bolshoi's repertoire on the other, then you must not forget that the success of any production and of any individual artist is linked with the honest development of the artistic principles which were laid down two hundred years ago and then enriched by the work and ideas of socialism in our country.

One of the main tasks of our company is to present contemporary life onstage.

Of course, the theater's repertoire must include the best works of the Russian national school—operas by Glinka, Mussorgsky, Rimsky-Korsakov, Tchaikovsky, Borodin. It would be impossible to picture the Bolshoi Theater without *Eugene Onegin* or *Boris Godunov,* without *Prince Igor* or *Ivan Susanin.* But time has brought with it new names which are winning their deserved place on the playbill. Of course, preference is given to works by Soviet composers. In the sixty years of Soviet power, more than forty operas by contemporary Soviet authors have been produced in the Bolshoi Theater.

It was not so long ago that Prokofiev's operas were the subject of great argument. Nowadays these works are a basic part of the repertoire, for instance, *War and Peace, The Gambler,* and *Semyon Kotko.*

There are indeed many contemporary works produced at various times by the theater that have been staged fifty or sixty times. These include operas by Shaporin, Shebalin, Shostakovich, Molchanov, Dzerzhinsky, Muradeli, Kholminov, etc. Among them there are those which are no longer being produced, but which nevertheless have left a distinctive mark on modern opera technique, and on those which are still appearing regularly.

Recently the theater has staged two operas by contemporary composers, *The Abduction of the Moon* by the Georgian composer Taktakishvili, and *Dead Souls* by Shchedrin, both of which were welcomed with great interest by the public. Who knows which of these productions will remain in the repertoire and for how long, which will be forgotten, and to which ones the theater will return once again in due course? Time will show. But it is clear that the line between the theater of proven classics and that of new works is becoming less and less obvious.

This can also be said of works by foreign authors. Britten's opera *A Midsummer Night's Dream* ran for several years with great success, and it is perfectly possible that it will appear again in a new production in the not too distant future.

Cooperation with authors on works dealing with contemporary themes is especially complicated and yet also very important. For a long time there existed a prejudice, which even had its own "theorists," who considered that an opera treating problems taken from everyday life must remain slightly detached and free from the mundane details of existence, and that its sentiments must be artificially exaggerated to compensate for the lack of these in contemporary life. Experience, however, has shown the reverse to be true. Our everyday life is a never-ending source of genuine passions, profound feelings, and subjects suitable for opera. The real problem, in fact, is that artists and directors in the world of opera are not always able to master the contemporary esthetics of theatrical production and are still using, as is the case of many composers who are unsuccessful in this field, the techniques of days gone by. Genuinely contemporary performance and the ability to recognize the true essence of life today—these are the keys which will open up the secrets of modern opera. It is a complicated process, demanding much patience and great experience.

After many long years of dedicated efforts, the Bolshoi Theater finally discovered the artistic truth which gave rise naturally to operatic forms of a very special kind. Its greatest successes in this field were definitely works about the Great Patriotic War, which express some of the most important events in the life of our country and the history of man. Dzerzhinsky's opera *Man's Fate,* Molchanov's operas *The Unknown Soldier* and *Here the Dawn Is Quiet* cannot fail to impress people today with their natural quality. They are exceptional in that they penetrate and express the real truth of deep-rooted emotions.

Themes from fifty years ago are already considered old-fashioned, yet very often they contain much that is relevant to contemporary life. It follows from this that contemporaneity does not necessarily imply topicality. In this sense Prokofiev's operas can be considered to a certain extent to be contemporary.

Opera singers of the seventies extend this sense of the contemporary to cover their approach to their own work. Their artistry consists in acquiring a thorough knowledge of works by modern authors, which helps them to become better actors on the opera stage and to become masters of the vocal and theatrical arts. It also makes them aware of the true natural qualities of the genre and its raison d'être. Opera singers ensure that their performance does not become in any way stereotyped by constantly remaining aware of and receptive to different situations in life itself. Thus they themselves learn to reject primitiveness, falsehoods, and pseudo-pathos. There are now noticeable signs in the classical repertoire of a new, more "truthful" approach in the work of artists who have at last ventured into the world of modern opera. We believe that the artist who confines himself throughout his career to the same dozen roles is severely limiting his own creative potential. Variety in roles, style, and type of production will broaden his creative horizons and will liberate him as musician, actor, and singer.

The new production of *Otello* caused great interest recently. This is an opera which contains fresh moral ideals, which are extremely relevant to the present day and age. These ideals are brought to us in the work of the Italian genius with international appeal, Verdi.

The best operas and most successful productions live on in the theater and run for twenty to thirty years. On the one hand they represent the sum total of the company's creative strength at any given time, and on the other they define the creative work of many generations of artists.

To quote an example, the present version of *Eugene·Onegin,* originally produced in 1944, has made a comeback every single season since then, and is nowadays being performed by third- and fourth-generation artists of the Bolshoi Theater. This helps make it possible to hand on a style of production while preserving its freshness and preventing it from becoming stale or stereotyped. This is the way in which acting traditions are developed.

Yet time takes its toll and productions that have become stale have to be readapted in new versions.

The repertoire is of course affected by the availability of certain performers in the troupe at any given moment. But its basic type of repertoire (Russian classics, contemporary works and Western European operas) remains unaltered.

What, then, is opera? Is it a play set to music, in which song replaces speech? A spectacle in which our ears are treated to the sound of the human voice? Is it a symphony concert taking place against the background of a painted set, performed by singers decked out in different costumes?

Opera, for us, is a drama expressed through music. All its elements—music, dramatic composition, poetry, song, theatrical design, set design, etc.—are means of expressing the ideas in works, which express life's truths and ideals. If just one of these means starts to become an end in itself, then the art of the opera will disintegrate.

In the light of this, the overall conception of the production, born of the mutual enrichment of classical works and the individuality of the contemporary artist, has assumed a vital role.

The genuinely great works of Mussorgsky, Verdi, or Mozart, Borodin, Puccini or Bizet, of Beethoven, Prokofiev or Rachmaninov, bring to each era its own fund of emotions and lessons to be learned.

Nowadays, with the help of the director, the artist can search for hints of contemporary outlook or understanding in the conceptions of the old school. Not only is he endowed with a modern way of thinking, but as a professional he has a better chance of understanding the author's meaning. If he develops a proper social consciousness of what his role should be, then a heightened artistic awareness and increase in artistic fantasy are born into the art as a whole, increasing creative activity and providing it with a better-defined framework and direction within which to work.

The classics are a never-ending well of knowledge. Their correlation with works depicting our life and times gives birth to the process of mutual enrichment, which is the basis of contemporary success. Every generation evaluates the classics differently; they speak to us in their own way as our contemporaries.

The Bolshoi Theater is the leading opera company in the country. It represents the banner of achievement in socialist arts and culture. The Bolshoi Theater is an example of the growth and development of the achievements of the great arts of opera and ballet in our country.

Boris Pokrovsky
Principal director
Bolshoi Theater

Mikhail Ivanovich Glinka

Ivan Susanin

Opera in four acts, five scenes, and an epilogue.
Libretto by S. Gorodetsky, revised by A. Pasovsky and L. Baratov.
First Bolshoi production on September 7, 1842.
In *Ivan Susanin* Glinka gathered together the sum total of other composers' experience before him and opened the way for the development of nineteenth-century Russian music.
Ivan Susanin, also known as *A Life for the Tsar,* can be considered the first truly national opera with its music in the authentic popular spirit.
The last version to be produced in the Bolshoi dates from 1945, when it was conducted by A. Pasovsky, directed by L. Baratov, with set design by P. Williams and choreography by P. Zacharov.

Opposite: Scene from Act I, in front of Ivan Susanin's house. A festive reception for Bogdan Sobinin, the fiancé of Antonida (Susanin's daughter), on his return from victory over the Polish invaders. Susanin consents to the marriage between Antonida and Sobinin only when the new Tsar is chosen.

Above left: A feast in a Polish palace (Act II). Together with the news of sudden defeat at the hands of the Russians comes that of the election of the new Tsar, Mikhail Romanov, whom the Polish leaders decide to kidnap. Above, right: G. V. Olezhnichenko (soprano) in the role of Antonida.

Above: A. F. Vedernikov (bass) in the role of Ivan Susanin. Opposite, above left: Antonina Vasilievna Nezhdanova, a great opera singer, in the role of Antonida. Above right: In Ivan Susanin's hut (Act III). The Poles force their way in and force him to guide them to the Tsar's hideout.

Below: Sketch by P. V. Williams for the 1939–41 production of Ivan Susanin. *On the following pages: Scene on Red Square. Epilogue. At the cost of his own life, Susanin has saved the Tsar. The crowd acclaims the liberation of Russia from the invaders and the deliverance of their sovereign.*

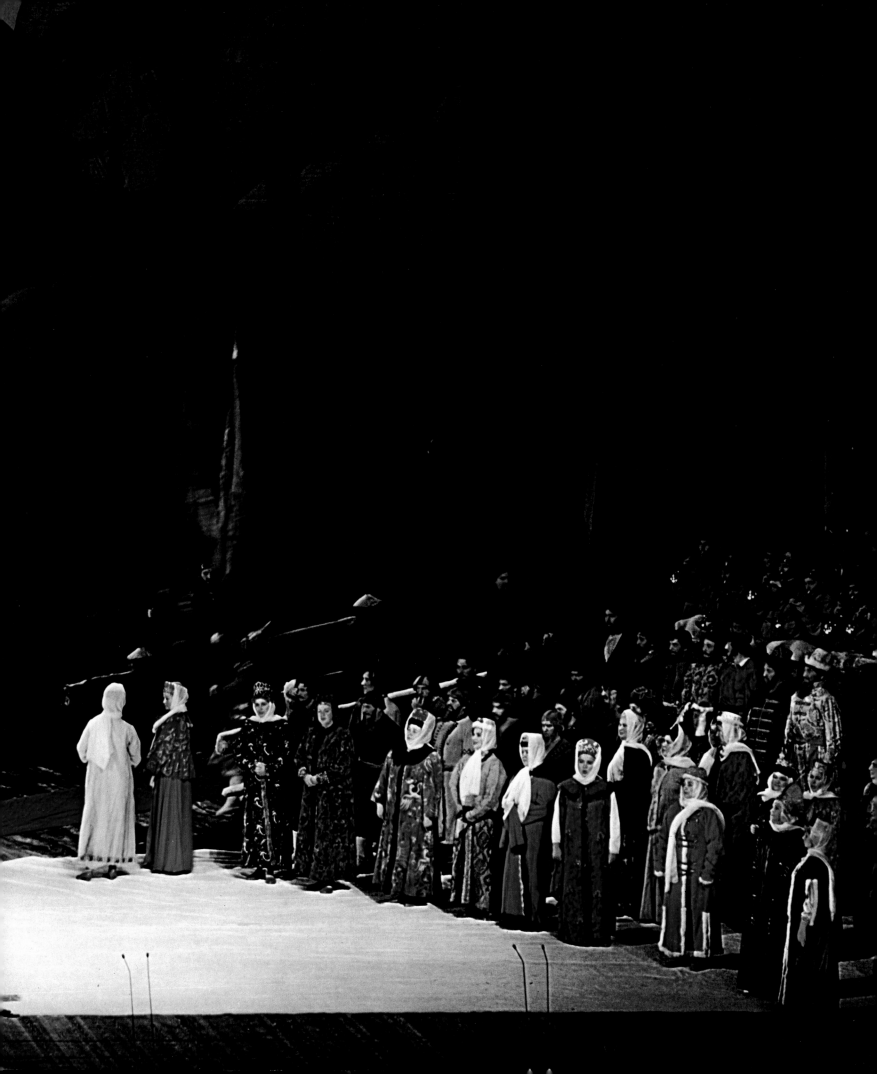

Mikhail Ivanovich Glinka

Russlan and Ludmilla

Opera in three acts. Libretto by M. Glinka and V. Shirkov after the poem by Alexander Pushkin, from which it takes its title.

First Bolshoi Theater production was on December 9, 1846.

The principal idea of the opera is that man can achieve genuine happiness only if he has had to fight for it. It is an epic opera, combining the strength of the epic poem with the poetry of the fairy tale.

The present version dates from 1972. Conductor: Y. Simonov; director: B. Pokrovsky; set designer: Y. Sumbatashvili; choreographer: Y. Grigorovich.

Left: Scene from Act I. Russlan, who together with his rivals Farlaf and Ratmir is searching for Ludmilla (daughter of Svetosvar, Grand Duke of Kiev, kidnapped by the dwarf Chernomor), arrives in front of a huge head which, when it breathes, creates a great wind. Transfixing the head, Russlan finds the sword with which he will be able to slay the dwarf.

Top: The odalisques' ball (Act II), during which the witch Naina tries to enchant Russlan and distract him from his purpose. But the magician Finno, who was at one time in love with Naina, arrives and breaks the spell, allowing Russlan to continue his search for Ludmilla, the girl he loves.

Above left: Scene in Chernomor's garden from Act III. Ludmilla, separated from her father and held prisoner by the dwarf, is sad despite the animated show of oriental dancing that Chernomor has organized to cheer her up. Above right: K. G. Kadinskaya (soprano) in the role of Ludmilla.

Opposite: B. A. Rudenko (soprano) in the role of Ludmilla, and E. E. Nesterenko in the role of Russlan. Above, from left to right: A. A. Eisen (bass) in the role of Farlaf; N. N. Grigoreva (contralto) in the role of Ratmir; A. D. Maslennikov (tenor) in the role of Finno the magician.

Top: Scene from Act III. Ludmilla is awakened by Russlan from a deep sleep induced by Chernomor. On the following two pages: Last scene from Act III, in which the people of Kiev celebrate the reunion of Russlan and Ludmilla after many ordeals overcome by the gallant young man in order to free his loved one.

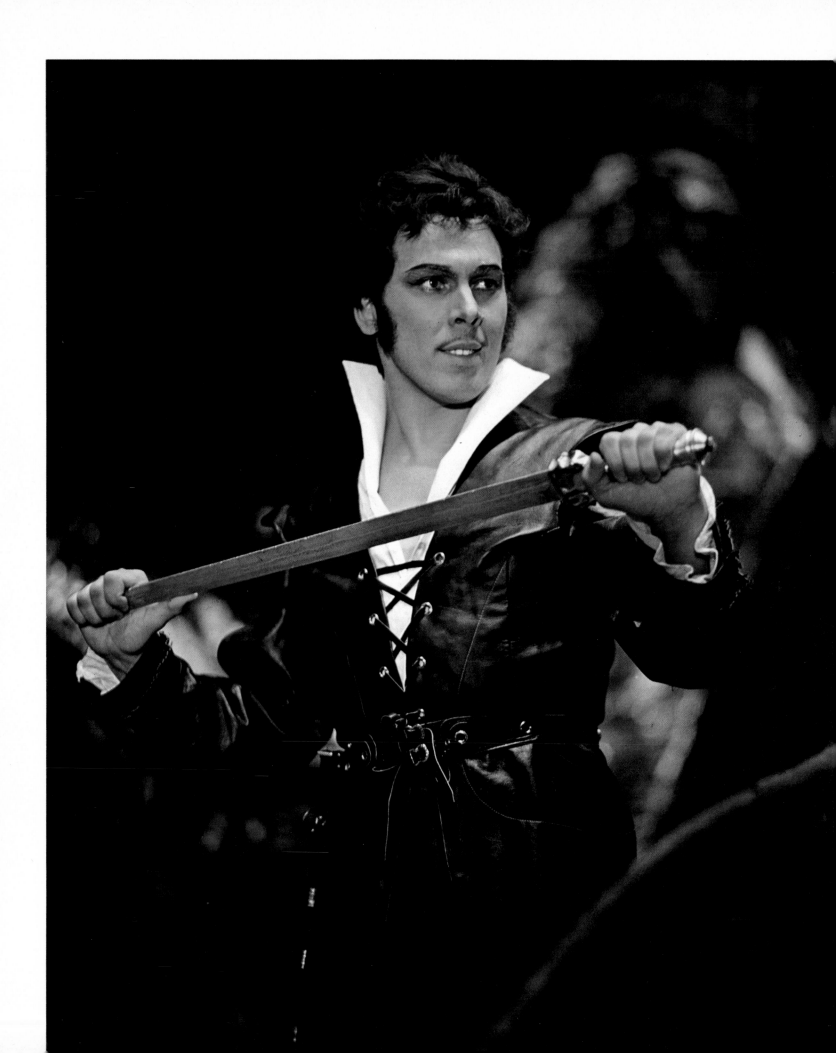

Giuseppe Verdi

Il Trovatore

Opera in four acts and eight scenes. Libretto by S. Cammarano after the drama of the same name by A. G. Gutiérrez.

First produced at the Teatro Apollo, Rome, on January 19, 1853, and at the Bolshoi on January 7, 1859.

Together with *Rigoletto* and *La Traviata, Il Trovatore* is a work in which Verdi shows himself to be a courageous reformer and a realistic psychologist.

Present version produced at the Bolshoi in 1972. Conductor: F. Mansurov; director: E. Fischer; set designer: N. Zolotarev.

Opposite: V. I. Pyavko (tenor) in the role of the troubadour Manrico, and, top right, Y. A. Mazurok (baritone) in the costume of Count di Luna. The photographs on this page are of the 1972 production, with set design by N. N. Zolotarev, directed by E. Fischer.

Above: Scene showing the chapel of the monastery to which Leonora, believing Manrico to be dead, has retired to take the veil. Her retirement is disturbed, however, by the Count di Luna, who rushes in determined to take her back. But Manrico also arrives and succeeds in snatching the lady from his rival.

Top: The gypsy encampment. Azucena, holding the wounded Manrico in her arms, is relating how her mother, accused of being a witch, was burned at the stake and died unavenged by command of the old Count di Luna.

Above, from left to right: Manrico and Leonora's duet; played respectively by V. I. Pyavko (tenor) and T. A. Malishkina (soprano); I. K. Arkhipova (contralto) in the dramatic role of the gypsy Azucena; the severe figure of Y. A. Gulyayev (baritone), in the role of di Luna.

Charles Gounod

Faust

Opera in a prologue, four acts, and six scenes.
Libretto by J. Barbier and M. Carré after the
dramatic poem of the same name by Goethe.
First produced at the Théâtre Lyrique on March 19,
1859, and at the Bolshoi on November 10, 1866.
Thanks to its poetic figures, beautiful melodies, and
elegant forms, *Faust* has become deservedly well
known.
The opera is not remarkable for the grandeur of its
ideas, profundity, or dramatic qualities, but has
become popular for its melodiousness, simplicity,
and natural expression.
Present version produced in 1969. Conductor: B.
Khaikin; director: O. Moralev; set designer: V.
Ryndin.

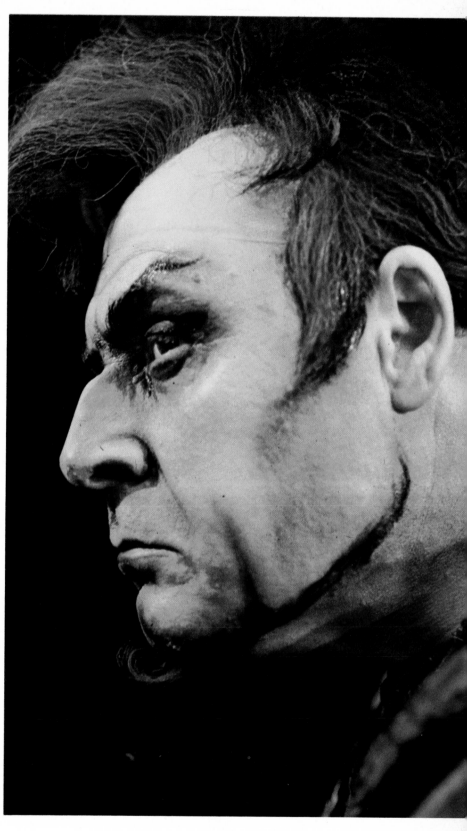

*Above: A. P. Ognivchev (bass) in a Mephistopheles mask. Left: E. T.
Raikov (tenor), in the role of Faust. Following the great success of the
opera, the composer turned the "spoken parts" into recitative,
transforming* Faust *from an* opéra-comique *into grand opera.*

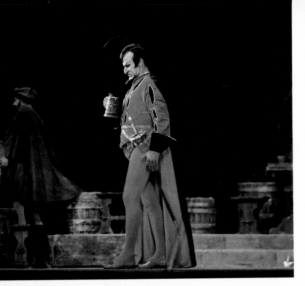

Top: In the six pictures from left to right, some of the great performers who have appeared in various productions of the opera at the Bolshoi Theater: E. E. Nesterenko (bass) in the role of Mephistopheles; A. A. Eisen (bass) in the same role; A. A. Eisen again in the devil's robes of Mephistopheles, while preaching disgrace to Siebel, played by G. S.

Koroleva (mezzo-soprano); A. A. Bolshakov (baritone), in the role of Valentin, addresses T. A. Sorokina (soprano), who is in Margherita's costume; L. M. Vernigora, also in the role of Mephistopheles; M. A. Miglau in the role of Margherita and A. S. Arkhipov (tenor) in the role of Faust.

Above: A double plate showing the scene from Act I which takes place in the village square in front of the tavern. The people are celebrating their countrymen's departure for the war. Valentin commends his sister Margherita to the care of his friend Siebel, who loves the maid to whom Faust is also attracted. Mephistopheles, in order to impress

his protégé, provokes Valentin into challenging him to a duel, but casts a spell making the blade of the young man's sword break as he holds it. Valentin, however, by seizing the sword hilt and holding it before him like a cross, succeeds in getting the better of his rival, who draws back, wrapping his red cloak around himself.

Above: An extract from Walpurgis Night. In the foreground V. V. Romanenko (Bacchus) is holding R. S. Struchkova (bacchante). Mephistopheles, in order to distract Faust from his remorse at having seduced Margherita and slain Valentin, takes him to an orgy in which the most famous courtesans from history are taking part.

Giuseppe Verdi

Aida

Opera in four acts and seven scenes. Libretto by
Antonio Ghislanzoni.
First produced in Cairo on December 24, 1871, and at
the Bolshoi Theater on March 14, 1879.
In *Aida,* apart from the lyrical side of the question of
love and devotion to one's country, Verdi raises the
question of honesty and steadfastness.
In writing *Aida,* Verdi, a profoundly national
composer, created music of worldwide significance.
Present version produced at the Bolshoi in 1951.
Conductor: A. Melik-Pashayev; director: B.
Pokrovsky; set designer: T. Starzhenetskaya.

Top right: E. V. Obrazhkova (soprano) in the role of Amneris.
Above: The temple scene from Act I. Radames' dream of leading the
Egyptian armies against the Ethiopians comes true; the commander
comes from the Pharaoh in charge of the armies which he will lead to
victory.

On the two preceding pages: The square of Thebes (Act II). The people are celebrating the triumphal return of Radames. Opposite: Detail from the above-mentioned scene: I. K. Arkhipova in the role of Amneris (on the throne) and T. A. Milashkina in the role of Aida. Top, from left to right: G. I. Borisova in the role of Amneris; V. I. Pyavko in the role of Radames; V. A. Valajtis in the role of Amonasro. Above: Palace scene from Act IV. Radames, accused of treachery, is going to be condemned to being buried alive. Amneris tries to persuade him to renounce Aida in exchange for freedom, but her words fail to move the warrior.

Peter Ilyich Tchaikovsky

Eugene Onegin

Lyric opera in three acts and seven scenes. Libretto by Peter Tchaikovsky and K. Shilovsky after the poem of the same name by Alexander Pushkin.

First produced on March 17, 1879, by the Moscow Conservatory at the Maly Teatr (Small Theater), and on January 11, 1881, at the Bolshoi. It is now regularly produced in many Soviet theaters and also abroad. Its music is outstanding for its surprising richness of melody. With *Eugene Onegin* a new type of opera was born in Russia, constructed not around interesting intrigue but around the discovery of the inner world of the protagonists.

Present version produced in 1944. Conductor: A. Melik-Pashayev; director: B. Pokrovsky; set designer: P. Williams.

Above left: Y. A. Mazurok (baritone) in the role of Eugene Onegin; above right: V. A. Atlantov (tenor) in the role of Lensky. Opposite: two scenes from Act I, in the widow Larina's garden. Above: Larina's daughters: while Tatiana sits apart, Olga celebrates the harvest with those who have gathered it.

Below: Tatiana, who is attracted to Eugene Onegin, invites him to a rendezvous. But the young man, who is the friend of Lensky, the fiancé of Olga, responds coldly to the young girl's proffered love. He tells her that he has an inconstant character and is not a marrying man.

Opposite: T. A. Kalinina (soprano) in the role of Tatiana. Above: A room in Larina's house, where Tatiana's birthday celebration is being held (Act II). Top left: M. I. Bocharov's sketch for the 1881–82 production of Eugene Onegin. Watercolour and pastel.

Top right: Duel scene from Act II. Eugene, to avoid being considered tied to Tatiana, dances too often with Olga, thus making Lensky, in a fit of jealousy, challenge his friend to a duel. Notwithstanding the two adversaries' initial hesitation, the duel takes place, and Lensky is mortally wounded.

Above: A ball in Prince Gremin's house (Act III). Six years have passed since the fateful duel. Tatiana has married Gremin and Eugene Onegin, invited to the party, on seeing her again, falls hopelessly in love with her. But this time it is she, faithful to her husband, who refuses the young man, although this only makes him love her more.

Opposite, from top to bottom: A. P. Ognivchev (bass) in the role of Prince Gremin; Y. A. Mazurok (baritone) in the role of Eugene Onegin, and T. A. Milashkina (soprano) in that of Tatiana; lastly, another singer who has portrayed the delicate character of Tatiana – M. F. Kasrashvili (soprano).

Modest Petrovich Mussorgsky

Boris Godunov

Popular musical drama in a prologue and four acts.
Libretto by Alexander Pushkin, after his drama of the
same name.
First produced at the Maryinsky Theater, St.
Petersburg, on February 8, 1874, and at the Bolshoi
Theater on December 16, 1888.
The score of *Boris Godunov* treats two main themes: the
social tragedy of the people and Tsar Boris's drama of
conscience. The sufferings of the people are expressed
with moving strength in the choral-lament passages,
and especially in the grandiose hymn of the
spontaneous peasant uprising.
Present version produced at the Bolshoi in 1948.
Conductor: N. Golovanov; director: L. Baratov; set
designer: F. Fyedorovsky.

*Above: Fyodor Ivanovich Chaliapin (1873–1938), the great bass, in the
role of Boris Godunov. Since Chaliapin's celebrated interpretation, which
became the model for subsequent versions of the opera, it is usual to choose
a bass for the part of Boris, although it was originally written for a
baritone.*

*Above: Sketch by F. F. Fyedorovsky (1883–1955) for the 1948
production of* Boris Godunov. *Opposite: A. P. Ognivchev (bass) in the
role of Boris Godunov. On the following pages: Scene from Act I showing
the coronation of Boris Godunov, a historical character who lived in the
sixteenth century.*

Opposite: A. D. Maslennikov (tenor) in the role of the Innocent. Top right: Scene in the Novodevich Monastery from Act I. Above right: Still from Act I, the cell of Brother Pimen, who is busy writing a history of the times, while the novice Grigory (the impostor) rests.

Top left: Once again from Act I, the tavern scene. The figure in the middle is the impostor Grigory (namely Dmitri) as played by V. A. Atlantov. Above left: Still in the tavern, A. A. Eisen (bass) in the role of Varlaam and L. A. Nikitina (mezzo-soprano) in the role of the hostess.

Top left: E. V. Obrazhkova (mezzo-soprano) in the role of Marina Mnishek. Top center: A room in Boris's imperial apartments at the Kremlin, from Act II. Opposite above: A. P. Ognivchev in the role of Boris and G. S. Koroleva (mezzo-soprano) in the role of Tsarevich Fyodor.

Above left: Tavern scene (Act I). Above right: A. F. Vedernikov (bass) in the role of Boris Godunov. Opposite below: Room in the Kremlin (Act IV). Boris, who feels death approaching, embraces his son Fyodor, naming him heir to the throne and advising him to rule justly.

The Queen of Spades

Peter Ilyich Tchaikovsky

Opera in three acts and seven scenes. Libretto by the composer's brother, Modest Tchaikovsky, after the story of the same name by Pushkin.

First Bolshoi production on November 4, 1891.

The opera has deservedly won itself a firm place in repertoires the world over as one of the most nearly perfect classical compositions. In the music of *The Queen of Spades* Tchaikovsky has achieved the ideal unification of opera and symphonic music. In the soul of the protagonist, German, there is a conflict between two feelings: his love for Lisa and the obsession to get rich; this is the basic content of the opera.

Present version produced in 1964. Conductor: B. Khaikin; director: B. Pokrovsky; set designer: V. Dmitriyev.

Opposite: V. N. Levko (mezzo-soprano) in the role of the Countess.
Left: Sketch by V. V. Dmitriyev (1900–48) for the 1944–64
production of The Queen of Spades, *which had 334 performances. Oil on canvas. Above: V. A. Atlantov (tenor) in the role of German.*

71

On the preceding pages: Scene in the garden from Act I. German, a relentless gambler, discovers that the girl with whom he is in love, but whose name he does not know, is Prince Yeletsky's fiancée.
Top: The ball scene, Act II. Lisa invites German to the house of the Countess, the "Queen of Spades," who is said to possess the secret of success in gambling.

Above left: T. A. Milashkina (soprano) in the role of Lisa and Y. A. Mazurok (baritone) in the role of Yeletsky.
Above right: Again Milashkina in the role of Lisa.
Opposite below: A moment from the ball scene with N. A. Lebedeva (soprano) in the role of Prilepa and I. K. Arkhipova in that of Milovzor.

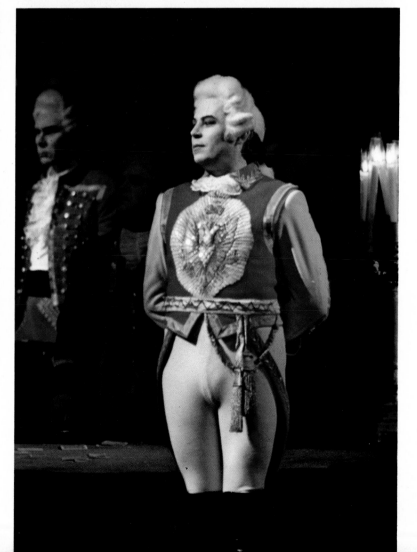

*Top: Scene in the gaming house from Act III. German, armed
with the secret extorted from the Countess, decides to try the
fate that will turn against him and lead him to suicide.
Above, left: V. A. Atlantov (tenor) in the role of German.
Right: Y. A. Mazurok (baritone) in the role of Prince
Yeletsky.*

Peter Ilyich Tchaikovsky

Iolanthe

Opera in one act. Libretto by Modest Tchaikovsky, after Henrik Herze's drama *The Daughter of King Renato*.

First produced at the National Theater of St. Petersburg on December 24, 1892, and at the Bolshoi on November 11, 1893.

The limited size of an opera of one act demands maximum conciseness and precision of expression on the part of the author. In this sense, *Iolanthe* is one of Tchaikovsky's most refined operas.

The version now in repertoire at the Bolshoi was first produced in 1974. Conductor: M. Ermler; director: O. Moralev; set designer: N. Zolotarev.

Top: T. A. Milashkina in the leading role. Above: an excerpt from the first scene. The action of the opera takes place in the middle of the fifteenth century at the court of King Renato in Provence. It is the story of the King's daughter, who, blind from birth, gains her sight thanks to the love of the cavalier Vaudemont.

Left: The finale of the opera with T. A. Sorokina in the part of Iolanthe and V. I. Pyavko in that of Vaudemont. Top: Sketch by N. N. Zolotarev for the set design, 1974. In tempera on posterboard. Above: V. A. Malchenko in the role of Roberto and V. A. Atlantov in that of Vaudemont. Iolanthe was Tchaikovsky's last opera.

Alexander Porfirievich Borodin

Prince Igor

Opera in a prologue, three acts, and five scenes.
Libretto by the composer after the ancient Russian
poem *The Lay of Igor's Campaign*.
First produced at the Maryinsky Theater, St.
Petersburg, on November 4, 1890.
The opera, full of love for the motherland, tells of one
of the brightest pages in the Russian people's struggle
against its enemies, the nomadic Polovtsy from the
steppes. A close study of folk song, a great love for its
creator, the Russian people, burning patriotism – these
are the characteristics which make up *Prince Igor*.
Present version produced at the Bolshoi in 1953.
Conductor: M. Zhukov; director: L. Baratov; set
designer: F. Fyedorovsky; choreographer: K.
Goleizovsky.

Above: Sketch by F. F. Fyedorovsky (1883–1955) for the costumes for
Prince Igor. *Watercolour, 1934. Left: The eclipse scene from Act I.
Igor, despite the eclipse, which augurs ill, decides to go out and meet
Khan Konchak's men in the open, as they advance on the city of Poutivl.*

Top: Scene in Galitzky's court, Act I. Opposite, above: Y. A. Grigoriev (baritone) in the role of Igor. Above: E. E. Andreyevna (soprano) in the role of Yaroslavna. Right: Scene in the apartments of Yaroslavna, who is anxiously awaiting news of her husband Igor (Act I).

Opposite, above: The Polovtsian encampment, where Igor is held prisoner (Act III). Below left: E. E. Nesterenko in the role of Khan Konchak; Below right: Y. A. Grigoriev (baritone) in the role of Prince Igor and A. F. Vedernikov in that of Konchak, leader of the Polovtsy.

Above: E. E. Nesterenko (baritone) in the role of Prince Igor. The plot of the opera was created by Borodin with the help of Vladimir Stasov, based on the oldest piece of Russian literature, the epic poem The Lay of Igor's Campaign, written by an anonymous poet toward the end of the twelfth century.

Above: The Polovtsian Dances. An autonomous piece, this musical extract is part of the world repertory of symphonic music and has contributed to the spread of the opera outside Russia.
Top left: A. A. Eisen in the role of Galitsky, brother of Yaroslavna, wife of Igor.

Top center: M. A. Miglau in the role of the maidservant and G. I. Borisova (mezzo-soprano) in the role of Konchakovna. Top right: Igor's return to Poutivl, Act III. Having escaped from the Polovtsian camp, he regains the city and is reunited with Yaroslavna. The people of Poutivl are no longer in danger; Igor will defend the city from the Polovtsy.

Georges Bizet

Carmen

Opera in four acts. Libretto by H. Meilhac and L. Halévy after the story of the same name by Prosper Mérimée. First produced at the Opéra-Comique, Paris, on March 3, 1875, and at the Bolshoi on November 27, 1898.
Carmen was composed in 1874, during a period in France which was characterized by the development of realism in arts and drama. This is reflected in the composer's attempts to penetrate, through the medium of opera, the emotions and thoughts of ordinary people.
Present version produced in 1953. Conductor: V. Nebolsin; director: R. Zakharov; set designer: M. Petrovsky.

Above: G. I. Borisova (mezzo-soprano) in the role of Carmen. Left: I. K. Arkhipova, also in the role of Carmen. The libretto, after a short story by Mérimée, notably attenuates the more crude and down-to-earth characters of the original.

87

On this page are some of the main performers in the different productions of the opera that have been staged at the Bolshoi.
Top: I. K. Arkhipova in the role of Carmen with V. I. Pyavko (tenor) in the role of José. Above left: E. V. Obrazhkova in the role of Carmen and V. A. Atlantov in that of José.
Above center: The soprano T. A. Sorokina in the role of Micaela and Z. L. Sotkila in that of José.
Above right: Mazurok (baritone) in the role of Escamillo.
Opposite: E. V. Obrazhkova in the role of Carmen. On the following pages: From Act IV, scene of the square before the arena; applauded by the crowd, Escamillo has arrived with Carmen.

Top: Sketch for the scene in the tavern of Lillas Pastia (Act II) by
I. F. Savitsky from the 1898–1916 production. Watercolour on
posterboard. Bizet's masterpiece met with a negative response at its
Paris debut. Its great triumph was to come eight years after its
first appearance.

Above: Oil on canvas sketch by P. P. Konchalovsky (1876–1956) for
the final scene, which takes place in a square of Seville, before the
arena (Act IV). This design was used in the 1945–51 production of
Carmen. Opposite: Another view of I. K. Arkhipova (mezzo-soprano)
in the role of Carmen.

Above: A. A. Eisen (bass) in the role of Tsar Ivan the Terrible.
Opposite, above: The dramatic expression of A. P. Ognivchev in the
same role.
Below: Sketch by F. F. Fyedorovsky (1883–1955) for the 1922–36
production of The Maid of Pskov. *Oil on canvas.*

For The Maid of Pskov, *Rimsky-Korsakov based his libretto on a*
drama by L. A. Mey (1822–62), but concentrated more on the conflict
between the city of Pskov and the Tsar than on the character of Olga
(Mey's heroine). This is why the opera is frequently known under the
name Ivan the Terrible.

Nikolai Andreyevich Rimsky-Korsakov

The Maid of Pskov (Ivan the Terrible)

Opera in a prologue, three acts, and five scenes.
Libretto by the composer, after L. Mey.
First produced at the Maryinsky Theater, St.
Petersburg, on January 13, 1873, and at the Bolshoi
on October 10, 1901.
Rimsky-Korsakov has concentrated on the conflict
between the city of Pskov and the Tsar, Ivan the
Terrible, in the period of centralization of the
Russian state and the submission of formerly free
regions such as Novgorod and Pskov.
Present version produced in 1971. Conductor: Y.
Simonov; Director: I. Tumanov; set designer: V.
Ryndin.

Top: Scene from Act II with the arrival of Ivan the Terrible.
Opposite: Two interpretations of the tragic character of the Tsar:
left: by Fyodor Chaliapin; center: A. P. Ognivchev. Above: G. I.
Borisova as Nadezhda and T. A. Milashkina (soprano) as
Vera.

Above: T. F. Tugarinova (soprano) in the role of Fevronia. Opposite, above: Forest scene, in the environs of the small city of Kitezh (Act I), where Fevronia lives alone and content, surrounded by animals. But one day the wounded Prince Vsevolod finds his way there. The maid cures him and he falls in love with her.

Opposite, below left: T. A. Milashkina (soprano) in the role of Fevronia. Right: The people greeting Fevronia, whom Vsevolod, Prince of Kitezh, has brought to take as his wife. The drunkard Kutierna advises her not to become proud of her good luck.

98

Nikolai Andreyevich Rimsky-Korsakov

The Legend of the Invisible City of Kitezh

Opera in three acts. Libretto by V. Belsky.
First produced at the Maryinsky Theater, St. Petersburg,
on February 20, 1907, and at the Bolshoi on February 15,
1908.
In this opera, Rimsky-Korsakov has put into music the
idea which comes from far back in Russian history, that
there is nothing dearer than one's native land, that we
should love it more than life itself and not betray it either
in happiness or in sorrow.
The music is based on Russian ballads, transformed by
the richness of full orchestration.
Present version produced in 1966. Conductor: R. Glazup;
director: I. Tumanov; set designer: V. Ryndin.

Top: Scene showing inner Kitezh suddenly invaded by the Tartars. Fevronia is taken prisoner. Opposite above: Scene showing greater Kitezh (Act II), when news has reached of the Tartar aggression. Before going to meet the enemy, Vsevolod and the people pray to the Virgin Mary for protection.

Above: The city of Kitezh reflected in the lake (Act III). Seeing this wonderful vision, the Tartars flee in terror. Opposite, below: Final scene. No one has survived and the city, bathed in a white light, comes alive again in eternity. The wedding procession of Fevronia and Vsevolod appears again as the two of them are united forever by death.

Modest Petrovich Mussorgsky

Khovanshchina
(The Khovansky Affair)

Popular musical drama in four acts and six scenes.
Libretto by the composer.
First produced at St. Petersburg on February 27, 1886,
and became part of the Bolshoi's repertoire on
December 12, 1912.
Mussorgsky, a composer of the progressive school,
captured the spirit of the people and embodied their
sorrows and joys in his music.
Present version produced in 1950. Conductor: N.
Golovanov; director: L. Baratov; set designer: F.
Fyedorovsky; choreography: S. Koren.

Above: L. I. Avdeyeva (mezzo-soprano) in the role of Martha. Opposite above: Sketch by K. F. Juon (1875–1958) for the 1939–41 production of Khovanshchina. *Watercolour on posterboard. Right: Scene on Red Square, Act I. The arrival of Ivan Khovansky, leader of the archers and symbol of "old" Russia.*

Above left: E. V. Obrazhkova (mezzo-soprano) in the costume of Martha, a mystical figure belonging to the ranks of Old Believers. Left: V. I. Pyavko (tenor) in the role of Andrei Khovansky, son of Ivan, and I. K. Arkhipova in another celebrated interpretation of Martha.

Above: Scene on Red Square from Act III. The people are watching the banishment of Golditsyn. Ivan Khovansky has been assassinated and the Old Believers burned at the stake. The opera, which was unfinished, was completed and orchestrated by Nikolai Rimsky-Korsakov. A recent revision was produced by Dmitri Shostakovich.

Nikolai Andreyevich Rimsky-Korsakov

The Tsar's Bride

Opera in four acts. Libretto by the composer and I. Tyumenev, after L. Mey.

First produced in Moscow on November 3, 1899; first Bolshoi production on February 2, 1916.

The Tsar's Bride, with its profound search through the music to discover the heroes' thoughts and feelings, is a convincing stand by the composer in favour of the folk roots and realism and against the formalistic tendencies which were widespread in Russia at the beginning of the twentieth century.

Present version produced in 1966. Conductor: B. Khaikin; director: O. Moralev; set designers: F. Fyedorovsky and N. Fyedorovskaya.

Opposite: T. I. Sinyavskaya in the role of Lyubasha. Above: Sketch by B. M. Kustodiev for the set design for the 1916–24 production of The Tsar's Bride. *Watercolour on posterboard. Top, from left to right, and above right: The character of Lyubasha as interpreted by T. I. Sinyavskaya, E. V. Obrazhkova, and I. K. Arkhipova.*

Lyubasha is a maid abandoned by Gryazhnoi in favour of the beautiful Martha, who in turn has been chosen by the Tsar for his bride. Not resigning herself to this, Lyubasha does everything in her power to regain the man to whom she feels herself indissolubly bound.

Above, left to right, top to bottom: Four members of the Bolshoi troupe: B. A. Rudenko in the role of Martha, and V. N. Levko, G. I. Borisova, and K. V. Leonova in the role of Lyubasha.
Top right: Scene in Gryazhnoi's house (Act I). Below center: Scene from Act II.

Top left: Scene from Act III. Opposite below and on the following pages: The royal chamber (Act IV). Martha, now Tsarina, is dying slowly of poison which Lyubasha tricked Gryazhnoi into giving her, telling him that it was a love potion. Then Gryazhnoi slays Lyubasha and is thrown into prison.

Wolfgang Amadeus Mozart

The Marriage of Figaro

Opera in four acts. Libretto by L. da Ponte, after the comedy *La Folle Journée ou le Mariage de Figaro* by Beaumarchais.

First produced at the the Burgtheater, Vienna, on May 1, 1786, and at the Bolshoi on November 23, 1926. Together with *Don Juan* and *The Magic Flute, The Marriage of Figaro* represents the peak of Mozart's career as an opera writer.

Last produced in 1956. Conductor: B. Khaikin; directors: B. Pokrovsky and G. Ansimov; set designer: V. Ryndin.

Left: G. V. Oleinichenko (soprano) in the role of Susanna and N. A. Lebedeva (mezzo-soprano) in that of Cherubino. We are in a room in Count Almaviva's castle during Act I when Susanna, at the Count's approach, hides Cherubino, who is in love with the Countess, behind the armchair.

Above, left: The Countess's room (Act II); L. F. Bozhko in the role of Susanna, M. F. Kasrashvili in that of the Countess, and N. Z. Glazyrina in the role of Cherubino, in another production of the opera at the Bolshoi. Above right: E. G. Kibkalo (bass) in the role of Figaro, the Count's valet, promised to Susanna in marriage.

On the two pages following: In the entrance hall of the castle (Act I). Figaro arrives with a group of peasant women carrying flowers. They represent the gratitude of the people for the abolishment of the jus primae noctis, as Figaro ironically calls it, knowing that the Count is hoping to seduce his fiancée. The Count recognizes the allusion.

Giacomo Puccini

Tosca

Opera in three acts. Libretto by L. Illica and G.
Giacosa, after V. Sardou.
First produced at the Teatro Costanzi, Rome, on
January 14, 1900, and at the Bolshoi on April 27, 1930.
In *Tosca,* Puccini combined the lyrical and intimate
qualities of the opera with episodes showing the
Italian people's struggle for freedom and their fight
against police repression.
Last version produced in 1971. Conductor: M. Ermler;
director: B. Pokrovsky; set designer: V. Leventhal.

*Left: Scene in the church of Sant' Andrea, from Act I. T. A.
Milashkina (soprano) in the role of Tosca and V. A. Atlantov (tenor)
in that of Cavaradossi, Tosca's lover. Above: V. I. Pyavko in the role of
Cavaradossi. Opposite: T. A. Milashkina again during the conversation
with Scarpia in Act II.*

Top: Sketch by V. Y. Leventhal for the set design of Act I (1971 production). Above left: Setting for Act I, designed in 1930 by V. A. Luzhetsky. Above right: Valaitis (baritone) in the role of Scarpia. Opposite: Scarpia's apartment, Act II (Mazurok in the role of Scarpia and Kasrashvili in that of Tosca).

On the following pages: Prison scene from Act III. Cavaradossi, condemned to death, awaits the end. Tosca, having obtained a safe conduct for her lover, kills Scarpia in order not to accede to his desires. But she has been deceived. Cavaradossi is really executed and she then throws herself from the parapet of the prison.

118

Above: Ball scene, Act I. Pierre Bezukhov, his brother-in-law Anatoly Kuragin, and Prince Andrei Bolkonsky are all in love with Natasha. But the first two are already married, and the latter, whose love Natasha returns, does not have his father's blessing on a union with a young woman of inferior rank.

Opposite: Profile of M. F. Kasrashvili (soprano) in the role of the beautiful Natasha Rostova. The young woman's serene life will soon be upset by the invasion of Napoleon's troops. The destiny of the other characters will also be linked with the painful events of war and with the eventual Russian victory.

Sergei Sergeyevich Prokofiev

War and Peace

Opera in three acts and thirteen scenes.
Libretto by Prokofiev and M. Mendelssohn-
Prokofieva, after the novel of the same name by
Tolstoy.
First presented at the Bolshoi Theater on December
15, 1959.
Prokofiev does not always follow the canons of
classical opera in this work, but he has managed to
create an original opera which has contributed a
great deal to modern operatic art.
The 1959 production has remained in repertoire
until the present day. Conductor: A. Melik-
Pashayev; director: B. Pokrovsky; set designer: V.
Ryndin.

On the two following pages: Beginning of the battle of Borodino (Act II). War with the French has broken out, Andrei and Pierre have enlisted to fight Napoleon's armies. During the furious battle at Borodino, General Kutuzov decides to withdraw his troops and give the order to burn Moscow.

Above: Scene showing the burning of Moscow, Act II. The order agreed to by General Kutuzov and his officers during the Fili council (opposite, above left) has been executed: Moscow is burning. Opposite, above right: Still in Act II, the death of Andrei, wounded at the battle of Borodino.

Opposite, below: Finale of Act III. The Russian people celebrate the victory over the French. Pierre Bezukhov, having learned that his wife is dead and that Prince Andrei Bolkonsky has also died, comes back to Natasha in Moscow, in the hope of being able to marry her and to rebuild a serene life together.

Vano Ilyich Muradeli

October

A popular heroic opera in a prologue, three acts, and eight scenes. Libretto by V. Lugovsky.
The opera was first presented at the Bolshoi on April 22, 1964.
Muradeli, with his elevated romantic style, evoked in *October* the glorious deeds of the masses fighting in the great socialist revolution.
The production of 1964 is still running today.
Conductor: E. Svetlanov; director: I. Tumanov; set designer: V. Ryndin.

Opposite, above: Artur Eisen (bass) in the role of Vladimir Ilyich Lenin, leader of the October Revolution. Opposite below: Sketch by V. F. Ryndin for the 1964 production of the opera October. Above: V. A. Valaitis (baritone) in the role of Andrei.

Above: Scene at Razliv. A. A. Eisen again, in the role of Lenin. Top, from left to right: A. A. Grigoriev in the role of the young artist; M. N. Zvezdina in the role of Manyusha, and N. V. Novoselova in the role of Natasha. Opposite: Scene at Smolny (Act III); Eisen again in the role of Lenin.

Sergei Sergeyevich Prokofiev

Semyon Kotko

Opera in three acts. Libretto by Valentin Katayev and
Prokofiev after Katayev's story entitled "I Am the Son
of the Working People."
Semyon Kotko was first produced in the Bolshoi Theater
on April 4, 1970. Conductor: F. Mansurov; director: B.
Pokrovsky; set designer: V. Leventhal.
This production continues in the repertoire today.

*Top, from left to right: Scene in Kotko's courtyard, Act I; Nina A.
Lebedeva in the role of Lyubka; A. S. Arkhipov in the role of Mikola
with E. V. Obrazhkova in that of his fiancée, Frosia. Above: From Act
I, scene in Tkachenko's house, where there is a gathering of villagers. The*
*story of Semyon and his fiancée Sofia is set against the background of civil
war and the birth of the partisan movement. Their love, made difficult
by events, is also opposed by her father, Tkachenko, an ambiguous,
opportunistic figure, who does not want a revolutionary for a son-in-law.*

Above: G. Y. Andryushchenko in the role of Semyon Kotko. Right, from top to bottom: V. N. Petrov as Semyon with T. I. Sinyavskaya as Frosia; A. A. Eisen as Tkachenko; V. A. Atlantov in another interpretation of the character of Semyon Kotko, the young man who fights with such devotion for the happiness of the people.

Lyubka, Mikola, and Frosia are all Semyon's friends, living in the same Ukrainian village and sharing the lot of the partisans against the German invaders and against counterrevolutionary groups of the Central Ukrainian Rada, which, in the troubled period of 1918 and 1919, opposed Soviet power.

Sergei Sergeyevich Prokofiev

The Gambler

Opera in two acts. Libretto by the composer after Dostoyevsky's novel of the same name.
First produced at the Théâtre de la Monnaie, Brussels, on April 29, 1929, and at the Bolshoi Theater on April 7, 1974.
In the music of *The Gambler,* Prokofiev renounced closed forms and chorus; the main performer in this opera is the orchestra.
The production of 1974, conducted by A. Lazarev, directed by B. Pokrovsky with set design by V. Leventhal, is still in repertoire.

Left: A. D. Maslennikov in the role of Aleksei, the youth who, caught up in the fascination of the game, becomes its slave. Top: A. P. Ognivchev in the role of the general. Above, from left to right: G. I. Borisova in the role of Blanche; T. I. Sinyavskaya, G. Y. Andryushchenko and A. P. Ognivchev in the roles of Blanche, the marquis, and the general.

Top: Scene from Act I. Above, from left to right: M. F. Kasrashvili in the role of Paulina, the lady whom Aleksei tries to save by devoting himself to roulette; A. A. Eisen in the role of the general. Opposite: Maslennikov in the role of Aleksei. On the two following pages: The gaming house from scene seven, Act II.

The Gambler is an opera which presents the fate of deeply human characters whose spirit is traumatized by social conditions. It represents a sharp and cutting denunciation of bourgeois society, in which all the negative aspects are covered by a mask of superficial respectability.

136

THE BALLET

Generations of artists, ballet dancers, and choreographers
have assimilated the heterogeneous styles and accumulated
experience of dance and have given the muse of Russian ballet
its own unique character, famous throughout the world.

The Old and the New Hand in Hand

Over the centuries ballet has gradually developed into the art we know today, and has guarded its development rather as our ancestors guarded fire, passing it on from hand to hand. It is this which makes ballet different from most, if not all, other forms of art. It is not possible to compare the art of the dance and, for example, pictorial art or the art of the spoken word. The artistic genius of thousands of years ago is preserved for us in the wall paintings of Egyptian pyramids and the even earlier cave drawings. And the work of Leonardo da Vinci and Praxiteles, of Rembrandt and Rublev will remain forever for future generations to enjoy, as will Homer's poems in the oral tradition, Indian epic poetry, and Russian *byliny* (epic poems), not to mention the literary masterpieces of word and thought which were born after the invention of writing.

The "written word" of ballet and its use of imagery as a medium of expression gives us a fleeting, living art which exists only at the very moment of the creation of the image. It is true that in this respect it does not differ from any other type of theatrical activity, either dramatic or musical. However, drama has a script and opera has a libretto and a musical score in which the roles are clearly transcribed. But despite numerous attempts, no one has yet managed to write down a ballet score in quite the same way, as it has a composition and scenario quite unique to dance.

Today the chronicler of its history has to consider the new muses of the twentieth century, namely the cinema and television. This does not in any way imply that the history of dance is disappearing without a trace, being swallowed up like water into the sands of the desert. As with the history of all other things, it is written, based on documents, contemporary memoirs, critical articles. And like all history, aside from its external appearance, it has its own pattern, its own sequence of events, and its own logical development. Whatever the generally accepted stages of its history may be, we have not even attempted to separate them, as it is not just one or two episodes but the whole process from the very beginning right up until the present day that has formed the art of the dance, given it its unique quality and boundless possibilities.

Classical dance has formed many generations of artists, ballet masters, and teachers, yet it seems as though its origins have been lost in the thick mists of time. However, I never cease to be astonished by one particular paradox of time, namely, the continuous presence of man in history, which can, at a single stroke, sweep away the barriers of years and even centuries.

For example, I was taught in the School of Choreography by Alexander Viktorovich Shiryayev, and, thanks to him, the forties and even the nineteenth century were brought much closer to me, because Shiryayev himself had learned under Christian Johansson, a pupil of Bournonville, who, in his turn, was taught by the legendary Vestris (we have already reached the eighteenth century), who was a pupil of Noverre himself! Two and a half centuries of development, but only five names, and each of these closely linked with the next.

A similar continuity is to be found in the never-ending relay of expertise, knowledge, and experience that has contributed to the development of our art, enabling us, by assimilating the achievements of forerunners in the field, to look at past and present developments through new eyes.

Classical, academic dance, the product of the French and Italian schools, was brought into Russia, and in the middle of the eighteenth century the long process of setting up a Russian school was begun, which from the historical point of view was something very new. But this process, which started out as imitation, cannot be truly evaluated without a proper understanding of the place occupied by dance in the life of the Russian people generally. Amid the grey dust of ages, there are to be found various recollections and accounts about the existence of dances in Rus—pagan dances, ceremonial, ritual, cult, and folk dances. The spontaneity of folk dancing has long been in the Russians' blood, and not only as an emotional expression of simple and understandable primary feelings, but also as an artistic, figurative reflection of everyday life and man's relationship with man. From very early times this spontaneity has contained the two elements of spectacle and game—in short, of theater. The jokes and games of the *igrishcha* (old Russian: a festive gathering of local youth with songs and folk dances) are entirely original, with folk roots, and are very "down-to-earth"— what we today would call art!

Dance is an entertaining, theatrical activity, from early times cultivated in the courts of Russian princes and tsars. When classical ballet started to infiltrate Russia (of course, it was nothing like the classical ballet we know today), there was no shortage of people able to adopt it and establish it as an art on Russian soil, people who were subsequently to develop it further. Feudal landowners and members of the aristocracy, unknown and (often) orphaned peasant children who entertained their masters so prettily on the stages of household theaters—these were the people who laid the foundations of the art of dance in our country.

It is also important to remember that not all stage and theatrical dance came to us from outside. With their typical grandeur, the Russian aristocrats engaged the best-known teachers and ballet masters from abroad. They were welcomed to Russia with fabulous salaries and by responsive new pupils who were eager and quick to learn. It could be said that there is not a single great name among the fathers of classical dance that is not somehow or other linked with Russia.

Even before the Russian ballet became an entity in its own right, touring troupes from other countries were frequent visitors to Rus. There are records of such tours dating from the 1720s. Peter I especially encouraged visits by foreign troupes; it is he, in fact, who introduced modern European dances into Russia.

All this inevitably led to the foundation in 1738 of the first theatrical school in the Russian capital, St. Petersburg. Although the court favoured foreign artists, who satisfied both their vanity and their thirst for secular entertainment, once the school was organized the Russian ballet's system of study embarked upon the road of independent development in a very convincing way.

Forty years later the old Russian capital Moscow, thrust aside by historical fate and forced for years to stand in the shadows, ignored by the powers that be, was given a ballet school and theater. The holders of the government's privy changed, the theater buildings had to be rebuilt several times following fires, ballet masters and teachers came and went, periods of flourishing gave way to periods of stagnation and fall in popularity, but the Moscow ballet lived on, developing its own special character and style.

When we consider the onward march of history, how the Moscow ballet came to be what it is, then it is with pride that we recall those artists, true devotees of their art, who carried the art of the dance with them through the years. History often does not preserve many names. It is as if, among the mountain summits rising above the range, only the very highest peaks of artistic talent shine out, the names of Terpsichore's disciples who glorified her delicate and fine art. But there would be no dazzling peaks if the mountain ridges did not buckle down and heave together to raise themselves high. I do not know how apt a comparison this is from the geological point of view, but from the point of view of art it seems to be true enough. Nothing comes from emptiness, and artistic talent in any sphere of spiritual and artistic life is always based on the experience of previous searches, and at the present stage of development in art, it is likewise based on its future objectives as indicated by those of the past and present.

The recollections of those who lived during the early years of classical dance have preserved for us the feeling of what it must be like to discover a new art form, with all its attraction and fascination. Over the centuries the costumes worn have changed beyond recognition, the technique and mechanics of dance have improved enormously, the very esthetics of the choreographic production have changed, and yet there must have been something which united time, filled every minute of its progress with intransient and lasting values.

Many elevated and enthusiastic words have been written about dance, but none can compare in brevity, simplicity, and accuracy with one line written by Pushkin which contains the very essence of dancing: "A flight filled with soul." He found the inspiration for these words not in his poetic genius alone, but almost as if the genius of creative dance had given them to him. They were dedicated to a certain ballerina who was the darling of ballet audiences, and also to the muse of dance in general, who flies across time, and whose flight is beautiful and uninterrupted.

Since its infancy, ballet has been linked with the stage effects typical of its early years, such as ghosts, shadows, various mythical and mythological characters. It seems as though its very nature responds to some sort of wasting away and elusiveness of the human condition which cannot always be expressed by ordinary words and concepts. There are always secrets of some sort in art, and dance found its particular secret in the fleeting transition from one condition to another, in a kind of elevation and uplifting of feelings and unearthly remoteness from the realities and conventions of everyday life.

But there is nothing metaphysical or nonhuman about the soul Pushkin was writing about. This image is seen as a great well of feelings, in which appear not only the actual personalities of the heroines but also the national characteristics of Russian women, the eternal spirituality of love and moral beauty. It is not possible to trace in exhaustive detail how the traditions of folk dancing became interwoven with the academic canons of classical dance. But there can be no doubt that in Russia there existed a very close bond between the two. This link was not, of course, discernible in exterior signs, and as time went on, classical ballet strayed ever further from the original folk dances. However, the inner bond, reflecting the lyricism inherent in the character of Russian women, their innermost preoccupations, the very workings of their soul, by its utter sincerity gave the muse of Russian ballet its special novelty and attraction, which are quite unique.

When people saw how ballet was able to relate life in a manner which other art forms are generally not capable of, they began to consider it an indispensable art. It was born of the synthesis of many art forms—music, sculpture, painting, literature, and theater. It became an art in its own right when it finally broke away from the confines of what had already been mastered and established.

I think that the Russian style of performance, which was influenced first by the Petersburg and then by the Moscow school, provided the basis which subsequently brought such glory to our national ballet. It goes without saying that the style of execution is not by any means simply the totality of technical devices or the predominance of one method or another. If we can say that the style is the man, then this is just as true when applied to the style of artistic execution. This young art form introduced man onto the stage, with his preoccupations, his web of feelings and emotions, the workings of his soul; these creations on stage are now on an equal footing with the very noblest images produced by modern-day creative arts.

And, bowing before generations and generations of unknown performers on the Russian stage, we must unequivocally recognize that it was they who were the roots which generously gave sustenance and strength to the new shoots. Their labour was not easy and at times required sacrifice; life is short and their lives belonged to the nation rather than to themselves.

As far as the stars of the stage are concerned, Moscow could often hold her own against the capital. One of the most dazzling names in the history of our ballet is that of a Moscow ballerina, Yekaterina Sankovskaya, a pupil of the French dancer Félicité Hullin-Sor, whose career was intricately linked with the Moscow stage. Among her other pupils we find remarkable artists such as Daria Lopukhina, Alexandra Voronina-Ivanova, Tatiana Karpakova and Konstantin Bogdanov. Yekaterina Sankovskaya, however, created a whole new era in the development of Russian ballet.

She made her debut in *La Sylphide* on the very same day that the famous Maria Taglioni, who has since become a legend in ballet, danced the same part in St. Petersburg. Her name became synonymous with a vibrating and airy style of dance, and she herself practically became an inaccessible and inimitable deity. But the magic of her name and dancing did not have any adverse affect on Yekaterina Sankovskaya's art. Her success with Taglioni's repertoire was no less than that enjoyed by the brilliant foreign ballerina. This was above all due to the fact that she did not even attempt to copy the inimitable dancer. Sankovskaya's greatest contribution to the history of the Bolshoi and Russian ballet was that she did so much towards the creation and consolidation of the Russian school of dance, introducing the art of dramatic choreography, with its polished technique and attractive expressiveness onstage, into already established pieces. It was not without reason that in the 1840s they used to mention her name in one breath with the names of the great dramatic artists Pavel Mochalov and Mikhail Shchepkin. It was not without reason that Saltykov-Shchedrin, who did not always view ballet with a favourable eye, called Sankovskaya the herald of truth and beauty.

But if Moscow was lucky with its ballet dancers, it was not so lucky with its ballet masters. The Moscow ballet's renaissance after many long years of stagnation was linked with the work in the Bolshoi of a pupil of Didelot's, Adam Glushkovsky. Glushkovsky was largely responsible for the appearance on the Moscow stage of spectacles made up of several acts: he did not look upon ballet as a combination of dances, or as light relief halfway through an opera. It is to him that we are indebted for the first ballets based on Pushkin's works. His productions of *Russlan and Ludmilla* and *The Prisoner of the Caucasus* were triumphs on the stage.

Towards the end of the 1840s, Marius Petipa made an unsuccessful debut on the Moscow stage, which very nearly discouraged him from doing any work in the Moscow theater. Attempts to invite other foreign choreographers to Moscow also met with little success. The French choreographer St.-Léon stayed longer than the others. He was a man of contradictions who was far from consistent in his experimentation. He tried to bring into the theater all the technical innovations of his time, including lighting effects and anything else that could possibly be tried out as a novelty. Moscow, which was used to a special kind of expressiveness in dance, was not overly delighted by his innovations and resisted his attempts at turning dance into an end in itself, a sort of kaleidoscope of technical effects. And although St.-Léon's work obviously did leave some mark on the theater, he did not greatly influence in any way the progress of dance in the technical sense; he was just not the right man for the job of leading the Moscow ballet forward to new horizons.

The result of this was that at the end of the sixties and the beginning of the seventies, the Bolshoi Theater went through a difficult period. The company was very mercurial, not having at the time a permanent artistic director. It had, however, several excellent soloists, yet at the same time was losing its collective identity, and suddenly found itself heading towards a crisis.

One attempt made by the administration to solve the problem was to commission the new ballet *Swan Lake,* by the leading light in Russian music, Peter Tchaikovsky. Alas, despite high hopes, the ballet, which was directed by the Austrian Julius Reisinger, did not prove to be a great turning point in the company's fortunes, although it did run for seven years and thirty-three productions (which was almost a record for those times). The reason for its lack of impact was that it had been produced in a hurry, lacked expression as a whole, and therefore did not succeed in filling the company with inspiration. The main reason, however, lay even deeper than this: the ballet master was not ready to assimilate the new principles of ballet, and he did not know how to read Tchaikovsky's full-scale symphonic score, which was, musically speaking, unlike anything else.

However, at the beginning of the twentieth century, an event took place which was to define the future path and development of the Bolshoi Ballet for a long time to come. A young and very talented artist, a pupil of Marius Petipa, Alexander Gorsky, was appointed artistic director of the Ballet.

Through his personality, Gorsky did more than just bridge the gap between the nineteenth and twentieth centuries; Moscow had long lacked an artist of such scope and ability, who was able to understand that the choreographic theater was going through a decisive period and that the winds of change were blowing in Terpsichore's temple. A new era was opening up in ballet. The brilliant life's work of Marius Petipa was coming to an end. He was a man who not only was ultrasensitive to the requirements of the times but managed to meet them almost before they arose; unfortunately, his contemporaries did not always seem capable of understanding this. In St. Petersburg, Mikhail Fokine began experimenting, throwing down the gauntlet on the academic stage. The "Russian seasons" in Paris were running with great success.

Gorsky was the sort of artist who made his position plain through his work. Under his direction the Bolshoi's repertoire was considerably enlarged, and included the best classical productions of former years. Many of the ballets he directed himself, showing a preference for large ballets made up of several acts.

Under Gorsky the Bolshoi Ballet started drawing closer to the newly established Moscow Artistic Theater.

However, the work of one artist, even the most talented, could not save the theater from the winds of decadence and formalism which were prevalent at the time. The Bolshoi Theater slumbered in the midst of heated arguments over the future of the ballet, in which the opponents and supporters of modern theater found themselves in equal force.

The October Revolution saved the art of the Bolshoi Ballet and decided its future path. The Bolshoi Theater became the country's leading opera and ballet theater, the home of democratic Soviet musical-dramatic art. The theater was faced with a new task: the creation of a contemporary repertoire.

The life of every creative company is always filled with many problems, but without them art could not exist, as every solution found to every problem is in reality another step forward. Even the problems themselves are no accident, but are conditioned by the development of changing situations which demand a fresh look at artistic principles, the search for new, unjaded forms, and the clarification of artistic position. The progress of time cannot be halted. Time hurries on, sweeping along with it art and the whirlpool of events, throwing out new problems to be faced, new artistic criteria and exciting new prospects.

The main problem of any ballet troupe is to put together a repertoire. It is the one task which affects all aspects of the theater's creative life; it dictates the influence that the company will have on its audiences, its own method of organization, and so forth. The repertoire is, if you like, the company's face on the world, its curriculum vitae setting forth the abilities of its members, the scope of the work achieved, and above all the direction which the theater is taking.

In the repertoire of the Bolshoi Theater today, there are shows based on many different artistic principles, styles, and directions, including classics and contemporary works. This scope does not imply a lack of criteria or the acceptance of anything and everything. We try to find a compromise in problems of tradition and innovation, and look for new works based on old traditions; or rather we look for a synthesis of tradition, as the history of Russian and Soviet ballet is very diverse and we have an extremely rare and valuable inheritance which it would be shortsighted and unreasonable to ignore. This is not to say that we should not maintain a critical approach towards what we have inherited; otherwise there would be a risk of turning it into an untouchable absolute truth. The theater must not become a sort of museum, an exhibition of masterpieces. That is why at every juncture old productions must be reviewed and carefully updated, bearing in mind the aspirations and tastes of the contemporary theatergoing public.

It is hardly necessary to talk about the great inheritance left us by the nineteenth century. It is well known to everybody. It was Marius Petipa and Lev Ivanov themselves who laid the foundations of symphonic drama. It was in Petipa's ballets that classical dance found its ultimate scenic form, which is still predominant today.

The nineteen twenties also brought prosperity to our ballet. This is true above all in the development of the forms and traditional movements of canons, an enrichment of the language of classical dance. It is worth noting that at that time the still young Fyodor Lopukhov theoretically founded the concept of "symphony ballet" and produced the first practical experiment in dance symphony, thereby opening up the road to the genre of ballet productions not having a specific subject, which subsequently became extremely popular in the works of many eminent contemporary choreographers.

The twenties were a time of experimentation and daring projects. Not all of them were successful; some gave rise to controversy. But the search for three-dimensional expression in the work of Kasian Goleizovsky in Moscow, and the move towards different genres in Fyodor Lopukhov's ballets in Leningrad, the interest in imagery in dance, the attempts to create a production based on a combination of the principles of choreographic symphony and development of the dramatic subject, are certainly worthy of our most considered attention. Unfortunately, the best productions of that period have not survived and my generation was not able to learn from the productions of these outstanding masters. But the strengths and influences of tradition are many and various, and are handed on, sometimes almost imperceptibly, through the personality of the master himself or through productions by other choreographers into which they have put much experience from the past. In the productions by today's generation of choreographers the influence of Lopukhov and Goleizovsky can still be felt; these two have gone down in pages of history which it would not be possible to strike out and which have become an organic part of our world of imagery, of our circle of ideas and artistic experience.

It is a pity that works by these artists are not to be found in today's ballet repertoire; time takes its toll, separating us further from the past, and every production, even the most outstanding, inevitably reaches the point where no reviving or readaptation can possibly save it. Nevertheless, in the present repertoire of the Bolshoi Theater we preserve classical ballets, Mikhail Fokine's shows, and productions dating from the thirties and the forties in the genre of choreodrama. We do not want to abandon them as we are trying to deal with our heritage in the best way possible, again and again referring to our recent experience and comparing it with that of the past. It is easiest of all to abandon what seems to us to be old-fashioned. But we must be careful not to judge by our own preferences, but to ensure that we understand what the future prospects are.

There have been considerable changes in Soviet ballet over the past twenty years or so. They were dictated by life, which had brought forth a new generation of artistic methods which were, in their turn, put into practice by a new generation of choreographers and performers. Soviet ballet survived the change of generation. It is always difficult, even painful, to survive this process, and inevitably conflicts arise, especially in view of the fact that the present historical stage was preceded by a period of glorious achievement. Today's generation, as is the case with every new generation, once having declared its own position, then set about confirming this in the polemic with the old. At times this polemic is unnecessarily heated, but its value cannot be denied. As is well known, truth is oft born of argument. Some time was required before passions abated and it became possible to make a sober analysis of what had been achieved by our forerunners, and to evaluate the usefulness of their experience in further development and improvement.

The thirties and forties were marked mainly by the movement which historians call choreodrama. It is possible that this term is not quite exact—(the concept of drama is applicable to contemporary shows as well)—and it does not reflect the essence of the school as a whole. Choreodrama came into its own in the thirties and forties. During this time productions such as *The Fountain of Bakhchisarai, Romeo and Juliet, The Flames of Paris,* and *Laurencia* were created. The choreographers leading this movement were Leonid Lavrovsky, Rostislav Zakharov, Vassily Vainonen, and Vakhtang Chabukiani.

While they were developing the traditions of the grand spectacle with a story line, the exponents of choreodrama widened the scope of subjects possible for ballet. They turned to Russian and foreign classical works of literature and introduced into the art of ballet new methods of direction and a psychological approach to the discovery of real characters. The attention to precision of style and detail onstage and the harmonious combination of artistic design, costume, and sets—coupled with the interest in socially relevant and important subjects—pulled ballet out of the exclusive circle in which it had been, and into an area of art which is as concerned with its own influence and content as the former was with pure esthetics.

Choreodramatic productions produced a whole new generation of performers, exemplified by Galina Ulanova. She began her career in Leningrad and then became involved with the Bolshoi Theater. Ulanova, who was to continue in the footsteps of Anna Pavlova, remains to this day a ballerina in a class of her own and a sort of ideal actress on the ballet stage, having set the example for a whole era in the history of Soviet choreography. The traditions of Ulanova's art are truly the great traditions of Russian culture given to the world by the greatest artists. They are the traditions of Strepetova and Yermolova, Pavlova, and Komissarzhevska; Ulanova's place is next to these outstanding mistresses of Russian art.

Many years have gone by, but is it really possible, for example, to forget Ulanova's Juliet? Many ballerinas have interpreted this role since, among them the best known and most popular. But Ulanova's performance remains beyond compare; Juliet's fragile decisiveness, courageous vulnerability, passion, and submissiveness, her willingness to make sacrifices and to fight for her love—I do not know of a more complete or more psychologically intricate understanding of any of Shakespeare's heroines than Ulanova's.

The essence of Ulanova's art is to be found in the spiritual completeness of each one of her characters. Stanislavsky's famous words about the necessity of expressing "the life of man's spirit" onstage have been fulfilled in every way on the ballet stage by Ulanova. In this is to be found the great enigma of her art—its content, its raison d'être, its poetry and beauty.

Galina Ulanova's generation of ballet dancers was faced with fundamentally new problems demanding a thorough understanding of the stage and insight into the motives behind the protagonists' actions and into their sociopsychological makeup. There is no doubt that all this was of great significance to the development of the Russian theatrical school, which was always trying to perfect its scenic and dramatic expression.

The positive qualities of this particular movement did not compensate for its shortcomings, which had become patently obvious as the genre developed, and which had not been given sufficient depth of thought at the time. The gradual canonization of the form with no analysis of its pluses and minuses led to the emasculation of the progressive elements which had typified it at first. By the end of the forties, choreodrama had already reached a critical point; at the beginning of the fifties the crisis had not only failed to be resolved but had become even more acute.

Let us now consider what led to the fall of the genre, which tendencies were responsible for its comparatively brief existence, even though the best ballets to come out of it still remain with us today.

Choreodrama's contribution to the development of the language of dance and of the forms and dramatic devices of the ballet onstage was insignificant. New content demands new forms, but choreographers of the forties and fifties concentrated only on form. Paradoxically enough, the concern over content went hand in hand with a disregard for form. The search for forms, new devices, new means of expression, was naively identified with formalism. In this way the harmony of form and content which is so vital to life was destroyed, and the evolution of this movement only served to deepen the rift between them. But perhaps we should take a closer look and see exactly what is meant by form. This is a fundamentally important question, the answer to which mapped out, to quite a considerable extent, the subsequent development of our ballet.

Form in a ballet is, of course, the dance itself. We are talking about the three-dimensional form of a work which will reveal its content. Dance is the basis of ballet's dramatic expression. And although, of course, it is shortsighted to discount other forms of expression, for example pantomime and stage direction and so on, it is nevertheless true that dance is the most important single element.

All other devices and means are subordinated to dance, which, when possible, unites them in a harmonious whole. Dance is the strongest and most emotional of all the means of expression which ballet possesses, having been created and then having developed as an art form according to the rules of dance from which it originated. Dance is the very nature of ballet, its language through which deeper emotional and philosophical concepts can be expressed.

Choreodrama, however, crowded dance out; ballet masters who had no faith in its dramatic expressiveness and content value tried to identify the laws of popular art forms such as drama and ballet. They preferred the cut-and-dried mimicry of pantomime, considering that this better represented the language of everyday gestures than did the complex imagery and loaded meaning of dance forms. The subordinate position of dance in choreodrama led to a sharp contraction in the scope of the ballet theater, and the loss of important traditions from the past, traditions of men such as Petipa, Ivanov, Gorsky. Structural forms that had been its backbone for many years were cast aside as useless, as were grand, full-scale dance ensembles and choreographic suites. Following the trend in the dramatic theater, the corps de ballet became an anonymous mass. Choreographic art lost its own unique kind of imagery. The evolution of the movement, which proclaimed itself to be the only true one, served only to further reinforce these tendencies, and the choreographer's room for imagination became more and more restricted as he found himself gradually allotted the role of director instead of that of author of the ballet and creator of its dramatic content and dance score.

The fifties brought with them a change in fortune. Choreodrama, which had by then lost its dominant position, became the object of a veritable onslaught from young choreographers. Ballet masters who were conscious of the achievements of their forerunners started to take a deeper interest in the traditions of the Russian school of ballet at the turn of the century and during the first years following the Revolution.

The previous attitude towards tradition had distorted one of the main laws governing the development of art—its historical continuity. This arbitrary historical evaluation had led to an erroneous understanding of the theatrical process and great excitement over certain methods as though they had just been discovered for the first time. A period of this type was intrinsically false, since the historical and artistic characteristics of the genre known as choreodrama were to be found in productions by Fokine and Lopukhov, not to mention Petipa. It is surely more relevant and more valuable today to analyze each historical period in the light of both its merits and demerits. It is not worth overemphasizing the defects, and can be just as fatal to exaggerate its best qualities. An artist must have the capacity to be critical, as this helps him to clarify his own position. It is necessary to learn from the past, but not to accept blindly everything we find there. The best approach is one based on assimilation of past methods. Whereas choreodrama has provided us with fascinating examples of the highly professional art of the director, other historical periods have enriched ballet in certain other aspects.

As a continuation of what we have just said, it would be interesting to find out what problems ballet of today has had to solve, what is new at the present time, and what choreographers of the new generation have brought to the art. There is an aphorism that says: "Anything new is basically that which has been forgotten in the past." We find ourselves turning once again to Petipa in our efforts to revive the principles of the dramatic composition of "symphony dance," to Fokine in the flight for the unity of elements in ballet, and to Lopukhov, using him as our springboard in the process of working out new means of expression. In order to develop the principles of ballet direction, we begin by analyzing choreodrama. It seems to me that we are now in the era of synthesis of traditions, of drawing together and summarizing the experience of a long historical evolution.

The contemporary era of Soviet ballet, which began in the fifties, was formed in response to the requirements of the time. Ballets in which the choreographer expressed his feelings and thoughts through the exploration of the inner world of the hero and his conflicts with life came to take the place of splendid retrospective spectacles. Attempts to really penetrate and understand psychology have led to a new type of ballet having its own poetic language expressed through dance, its own metaphors, and a variety of philosophic interpretations. The monumental scenes have disappeared and the genre of the lyric poem has been revived. New forms of the traditional fairy tale and heroic ballet have appeared. All of this has led to the search for a new type of expression based on classical dance, embodied in the director's dramatic composition using the music and ballet.

It may be true that ballet has not produced any new subjects as it did during the period of choreodrama, but it has produced new heroes whose spiritual makeup and inner world are in sympathy with the thoughts and feelings of modern man. My colleagues and I see our main task as that of opening up the inner world of our contemporaries. There may be different ways of going about this, different methods of using one genre or another, but they are always based on past experience. There, in my opinion, is where the true essence of innovation lies—in the gradual familiarization with and comprehension of the past, and a synthesis of this, capable of giving it a new quality. Any innovation or search in general which ignores existing customs and traditions inevitably turns into pure dilettantism and endless repetition. In the search for synthesis, the artist's own position is perhaps more important than anything else, and also the position of the company as a creative body. Synthesis is not a mechanical thing: its basis is artistic selection, correlated with the requirements and esthetic concepts of the times.

An important trait in the contemporary life of the ballet theater is its rich variety of styles and genres and its individuality.

This is precisely why we in the Bolshoi Theater try not to limit our repertoire to any one type of production. We are equally in favour of comic ballets, dramatic ballets, ballets treating an important theme, one-act ballets without a theme, and ballets based on classical dance which use other three-dimensional principles. It is just as detrimental nowadays as it was in the past to favour and work with only one form.

Synthesis, then, should be capable of giving a new quality, a variety of styles and tendencies. But there are still other problems which are being tackled today. The most important of these is the eternal problem of art's relevance to contemporary life. What do we consider contemporary in ballet? Means of expression? Language of dance? Dramatic principles, the subject?

The conventions governing ballet often seem to stand in the way of contemporary subjects. Characters and situations taken from everyday life and real-life details somehow do not ring true on the ballet stage. But perhaps this has happened because the authors of such works have tried to overcome the poetic conventions of ballet by putting realism and the quality of being true to life in one and the same category.

Ballet is able to produce a poetic representation of life—not a literal one, but one that uncovers the inner essence, true character, feelings, and psychology—man's links with time. There are many difficulties to be overcome on the way towards working out the problems of the contemporary ballet production. So far there are no definitive examples of successful solutions. No doubt the choreographers and dancers are to blame for this, but so are the composers, librettists, and critics, all of whom are looked to to provide a theoretical foundation for the principles governing the approach to contemporary themes.

We often regard the concept of contemporaneity in a literal light, assuming it to mean only those ballets set in modern-day situations. But a ballet with a contemporary subject is not necessarily contemporary in essence. It is not so much a question of the quality of one production or another as of ballet's position in the theater, analogous to that of poetry in literature: with its traditionally romantic, fairy-tale themes, ballet is able to treat contemporary subjects in a much broader way. It seems to me that many people fall into the trap of confusing "contemporary subject" with "contemporary theme." They are not one and the same thing. It is not a question of the subject, but of the ideological and artistic structure of the work, the personalities of its heroes, the position of the choreographer, who is, after all, the author of the production, of what he wants to defend or argue with or put across to the audience. The artist's position defines the contemporaneity of the production. All this, of course, does not deny the fact that there are problems in ballets with contemporary subjects, problems which must be solved urgently, and it does not suggest that there are not other ways to search for a contemporary theme.

On the other hand, the fact that a ballet is set in the past does not mean that it is not relevant to the audience of today. For many long years now *Giselle* has been a part of the Bolshoi's repertoire, and every generation discovers something new in it. I am thinking not only about the audiences when I say this, but also about the dancers themselves, who bring to this eternal ballet subject their own fresh ideas and philosophies. We consider that one of our most honourable tasks is to preserve all of Tchaikovsky's ballets in our repertoire, as they are considered the theater's visiting card. The stage at the Bolshoi has already seen many different versions of Tchaikovsky's classical works, and I do not doubt that in the future people will turn more and more to Tchaikovsky's scores. The Soviet era has also created its own ballet classics, among the first pioneers of which was Sergei Prokofiev. Several of Prokofiev's ballets are still in the repertoire today, and his music will likewise never be allowed to fade from the Bolshoi's stage. It has become necessary to review some of the old editions, as the inheritance of the ballet theater is not only a choreographical one but a musical one as well. The development of ballet music has more than once outstripped the development of the ballet theater. This is why the preoccupation with the inheritance left to us by great choreographers and masters of the past must not be allowed to overshadow another, no less complicated, problem – that of careful attention to our unique musical scores.

The progress of Aram Khachaturian's *Spartacus* in our theater provides us with a good example of this careful attention to Soviet musical scores. This music has been presented at three different times in the Bolshoi Theater. The new productions of the ballet were created to satisfy the need to consider one of the heroic figures in world history from a modern point of view.

Recent ballets are also continuously in repertoire at our theater. Many of these productions are in fact the debuts in the Bolshoi of composers and ballet masters of different generations, different creative principles and styles.

It is only by having such a variety that life can be really full and creative. The Bolshoi ballet company, having begun its triumphant tours around the world in the fifties, is regarded today as a company which expresses the highest principles of art, which through the creative medium opens up to audiences the very soul of our people and their ideals. History never stands still. It becomes history only after the passage of a certain amount of time – and yet it is today when it is being written.

It is being written by the latest generation of Soviet actors, who have assimilated the rich experience of Russian, Soviet, and world theater. I am not going to give a list of the dancers at present in our theater – the reader will come across the leading stars of the Bolshoi company in the pages of this book – but I have no doubt that more than one of these names will eventually be written in golden letters in the history book of the Bolshoi Theater.

The tradition of continuity, of passing on one's experience, continues unbroken, enriching the art of the dance, opening up before it new horizons and new goals to be reached.

Yuri Grigorovich
Principal Ballet Master
Bolshoi Theater, U.S.S.R.

Adolphe Charles Adam

Giselle

Ballet in two acts. Libretto by Théophile Gautier and Vernoy de St.-Georges.
Giselle had its Bolshoi premiere on November 25, 1843, and since then there have been nine new productions. The leading role has been danced by the best Russian ballerinas, among whom Galina Ulanova stands out with her superb interpretation. The production at present in repertoire dates back to 1944. Choreography is by Jean Coralli, Jules Perrot and Marius Petipa, revised by Leonid Lavrovsky. Set design by B. Volkov.

Giselle is a typical example of the romantic ballet. Now, more than a century after its first appearance, it still figures largely in the repertoires of companies the world over. It unfolds a story dear to the romantic sensibility, a duality of love and death, and finds ample room for fantasy.

Top: Galina Ulanova (Giselle) with Mikhail Gabovich (Albrecht). Above, from left to right: Yekaterina Maximova in the role of Giselle; death of Giselle (finale of Act I). N. V. Pavlova in another interpretation of Giselle. Opposite: Marina Kondratyeva. On the following pages: Night scene from Act II.

Other dancers in the role of Giselle: (top) L. I. Semenyaka and (above left) N. I. Bessmertnova in the leading role; (above right) M. L. Lavrovsky in the role of Albrecht. The ballet relates the sad story of Giselle's love for Count Albrecht, a passion which leads to her death. Before her tomb, the maid is called back from the dead by the Queen of the Wilis, the spirits of maidens who died of broken hearts, whose destiny it is to lead men to their ruin. When Albrecht reaches the tomb to place flowers upon it, the Queen orders Giselle to dance with him until he dies. But the maid protects him until the morning, when the Wilis lose their power.

Leon Minkus

Don Quixote

Ballet in three acts and seven scenes. Libretto after Miguel Cervantes. First produced at the Bolshoi Theater on December 14, 1869, under the direction of the great choreographer Marius Petipa, but in 1900 Alexander Gorsky rechoreographed it, and the new version is the one at present in repertoire. The present version of the ballet was produced in 1940 when new dances by Kasian Goleizovsky and Rostislav Zakharov were included. Set design by Vadim Ryndin.

Top: M. L. Lavrovsky in the role of Basilio with the talented Nina Timofeyeva in the role of Kitri. Above: Sketch for the February 1940 production of Don Quixote.
Left: Another interpretation of Basilio by Maris Liepa.

155

Opposite, above: The celebrated character actor Yaroslav Sekh in the role of the toreador. Opposite below: Bessmertnova, noted for her delicacy and femininity, in the role of Kitri. Above: The scene of Don Quixote's dream, Act II. In the ballet, dance and music predominate over the story line. On the following pages: The ball in the Duke's palace. In the foreground: Kitri, Basilio, Don Quixote, and Sancho Panza.

Peter Ilyich Tchaikovsky

Swan Lake

Ballet in three acts and four scenes. Libretto by V. P. Begichev and Vasily Geltzer.

Swan Lake is one of Tchaikovsky's best-loved works and is considered to be the beginning of Russian ballet. It was first produced at the Bolshoi Theater in 1877. Eight different productions followed, the last of which was presented in 1969. This version, which continues in repertoire, has choreography by Yuri Grigorovich, including fragments by Lev Ivanov, Marius Petipa and Alexander Gorsky, with set design by S. Virsaladze.

Opposite, above: L. I. Semenyaka in the role of Odile and A. B. Godunov in that of the Prince. Opposite, below, from left to right: M. M. Plisetskaya in the role of Odile and N. B. Fadeyechev in that of the Prince; T. N. Golikova (Odette) and A. B. Godunov (the Prince); I. A. Kolin, A. B. Godunov and I. S. Vasiliev in the pas de trois.

Above: The great Plisetskaya in the role of Odette, the unhappy maiden who, put under a spell by the magician Rothbart, is a swan by day and returns to her human form by night. Only the Prince, by rejecting the magician's daughter Odile and proving his faithful love for Odette, succeeds in freeing her from the curse.

Opposite: N. I. Bessmertnova in the role of Odette and A. B. Godunov in the role of the Prince. Above: M. M. Gabovich in the role of the Evil Genius (the magician Rothbart). Top left and above right: Sketches by S. B. Virsaladze for the sets and costumes of the 1969 production of Swan Lake.

*Nocturnal scene on the lake shore, Act IV. The swan maidens weave
a sad dance expressing the suffering of their queen Odette, who
mistakenly believes herself betrayed. The Prince, on the contrary,
through his great love for her, is able to free her from the spell which
the magician Rothbart had cast on her.*

Peter Ilyich Tchaikovsky

The Sleeping Beauty

Ballet in three acts with a prologue and apotheosis.
Libretto by Ivan Vsevolozhsky and Marius Petipa
after the fairy tale by Charles Perrault. This is one of
Tchaikovsky's most sparkling, festive, and lively
works. The ballet exalts the triumph of life over
death, of sun over darkness, of the goodness of love
over evil and villainy.
Its first Bolshoi production took place in 1899,
which means that it has been running on this stage
for eighty years, in seven different productions. The
version at present in repertoire dates from 1973.
Yuri Grigorovich has made a cautious return to the
earlier choreography of Marius Petipa, updated in
line with today's tastes and advances in
contemporary art. Set design by S. Virsaladze.

Opposite: L. I. Semenyaka in the role of Princess Aurora. Above left:
A. Y. Kondratov in the role of Blue Bird and I. S. Prokofieva in
that of Princess Florina. Above right: Apotheosis scene from Act III.
Florimund, who has awakened Aurora from a long sleep, dances
with her.

167

On the preceding pages: The Waltz of the Flowers from Act I.
During Aurora's sixteenth birthday party, the prediction made by
the fairy Carabosse that the maiden will fall into a deep sleep lasting
a hundred years comes true. Above: V. V. Vasiliev in the role of the
Prince Désiré and Yekaterina Maximova in the role of Aurora.

Alexander Glazunov

Raymonda

Ballet in three acts. Libretto by Leonid
Lavrovsky, after a medieval Hungarian legend
about the White Lady.
Raymonda first appeared at the Bolshoi Theater
on January 23, 1900 with choreography by
Marius Petipa. In 1908 the ballet was
rechoreographed by Alexander Gorsky. The third
version by Lavrovsky was produced in 1945.

Top: Scene from the ballet Raymonda. *Above: Sketch by S. S.*
Kobuladze for the 1945–66 production of Raymonda. *Oil on*
canvas. The ballet relates the story of Raymonda's love for Jean de
Brienne, who returns from war in time to protect the woman he
loves from the machinations of the Saracen.

171

Left: Scene from the ballet with M. M. Plisetskaya in the role of Raymonda. Above, from top to bottom: E. L. Ryabinkina in the role of Raymonda; M. E. Liepa as Jean de Brienne, with R. K. Karelskaya as Raymonda; E. L. Ryabinkina again, in the same role.

Peter Ilyich Tchaikovsky

The Nutcracker

Ballet in two acts. Libretto by Lev Ivanov, revised by
Yuri Grigorovich, after the tale by E. T. A. Hoffmann.
The ballet was first produced in St. Petersburg in 1892
and did not appear in the Bolshoi until after the
October Revolution, on May 21, 1919, with
choreography by Alexander Gorsky and set design by
Constantine Korovine, who decided to interpret it as a
show for children.
The version at present in repertoire dates from 1966.
Yuri Grigorovich has restored the original score and
libretto to the ballet, as designed but never put into
practice by the great choreographer Marius Petipa. The
stage design of the present version is based on sketches
by S. Virsaladze.

Opposite, above: N. I. Bessmertnova in the role of Masha. Opposite, below left: V. M. Gordeyev in the role of the Prince and N. V. Pavlova in that of Masha. Opposite, below right: In the role of Masha, Yekaterina Maximova, who joined the Bolshoi School in 1949, graduated from it in 1958, and soon became famous the world over.

Above: Yekaterina Maximova, again in the role of Masha, the little girl whose godfather, a toymaker, gives her a nutcracker in the form of a soldier for Christmas. When Masha falls asleep, the nutcracker, in her dream, changes into a prince and the two dance with fairy-tale characters and toys that have come to life.

Opposite: M. L. Lavrovsky in the role of the Prince. Above left (from top to bottom): three scenes from the Dance of the Dolls: the Spanish Dance performed by I. A. Lazareva and M. L. Chivin, the Chinese Dance with E. V. Bunina and S. Yagudin; the Russian Dance with V. L. Antonov and T. L. Cherkasskaya.

Above right: Yekaterina Maximova in the role of Masha and V. V. Vasiliev in the role of the Prince. On the following pages: The final adagio. The Nutcracker has an important place in the history of modern ballet because Tchaikovsky introduced into it symphony motifs which blended in with traditional ballet music.

177

Top: Sketch by M. I. Kurilko (1880–1969) for the 1949–54
production of The Red Poppy; oil on canvas. Above: Port scene
from Act I. Events in the ballet are centered on the dancer Tao Hoa,
who sacrifices her own life in order to save the leader of a
revolutionary group.

Reinhold Glière

The Red Poppy

Ballet in three acts and thirteen scenes.
Libretto by Mikhail Kurilko and Vasily
Tikhomirov. *The Red Poppy* was the first ballet
on a contemporary theme to be produced on
the stage of the Bolshoi Theater. The ballet
describes the condition of the Chinese workers
in the twenties. It was first produced on June
14, 1927 with choreography by Tikhomirov
and Lev Lashchilin, leading roles danced by
such eminent dancers as Yekaterina Geltzer
and Tikhomirov. Later Galina Ulanova
created an unforgettable Tao Hoa, the main
character in the story.

*Left: G. S. Ulanova in the role of the dancer Tao Hoa. Top: S. G.
Koren in the role of Shang-fu, the mean capitalist, and G. S.
Ulanova as Tao Hoa. Above: the Acrobat's Dance from Act III, as
performed by G. K. Farmaniantz. This is one of the many dances for
which this ballet is famous.*

*Above: M. V. Kondratyeva, M. E. Liepa, and E. M. Matveyeva.
Opposite, from top to bottom: Two dancers of the past, Galina
Sergeyevna Ulanova and B. I. Khoklov. Ulanova, who graduated
from ballet school in 1928, joined the Bolshoi Ballet in 1935. Her
last stage appearance was in 1962; she has since remained with the
Bolshoi as a ballet mistress.*

Frédéric Chopin

Chopiniana
(Les Sylphides)

Ballet in one act. *Chopiniana* was produced by
Mikhail Fokine, the celebrated choreographer,
reformer and innovator at the beginning of the
century. The first dancer to perform it was the
famous ballerina Anna Pavlova, who took it to Paris
with huge success during the Russian Ballet's 1909
visit to the French capital.
Chopiniana was first produced at the Bolshoi in 1932
and still runs today in the 1958 version with
choreography by Alexander Gorsky and set design
by Vadim Ryndin. The ballet does not have a
definite subject, but following Chopin's music it
leads the audience into the poetic world of the great
romantic composer.

Opposite: G. V. Kozlova, V. P. Tikhonov and T. N. Golikova. Above: A scene from the ballet in which the dancers put on the long white tutu made famous by the Italian ballerina Maria Taglioni, who wore it in Schneitzhoeffer's La Sylphide, *from which* Chopiniana *has borrowed its name.*

From the ballet Chopiniana, *which was first given at the Maryinsky Theater, St. Petersburg, in March 1908, and appeared in a second production in April of the same year. It was first presented before Parisian audiences at the Théâtre de Chatelet in 1909. Outside Russia, the ballet is generally known under the name* Les Sylphides.

Boris Vladimirovich Asafiev

The Fountain of Bakhchisarai

Ballet in four acts with prologue and epilogue.
Libretto by Nikolai Volkov after the poem by
Alexander Pushkin.
The Fountain of Bakhchisarai was produced in 1936
with choreography by Rostislav Zakharov and set
design by Valentina Khodasevich. From the very
beginning it has had great success. Notable among
those who have performed in it are Galina Ulanova,
who interpreted the role of Maria, and Maya
Plisetskaya in the role of Zarema. The story is that of
an attack by the Crimean Tartars against Russia. It is
the first Soviet ballet based on a poem by the founder
and great poet of Russian literature, Pushkin.

*Opposite: M. V. Kondratyeva in the role of Maria. Top: from
Act I, ball in the garden of the Polish Prince in honour of his
daughter Maria's birthday. The party is interrupted by the
Tartar Khan Guirei, who is in love with Maria and abducts her
after stabbing her fiancé.*

*Above: Guirei's harem, from Act II. Zarema, who at one time
enjoyed Guirei's favour, is trying to rekindle his love. But the
Khan thinks only of Maria, and Zarema, mad with jealousy,
slays her rival. Center: The internal courtyard from Act IV.
Despite the arrival of new slaves for the harem, Guirei cannot
forget Maria.*

187

Above: Scene from Act IV. V. I. Kozhadei in the role of Nural, a Tartar who performs a wild dance to distract the Khan from his suffering. Opposite: The epilogue. The inconsolable Guirei in front of the Fountain of Tears, which he has erected in memory of his lost Maria.

Sergei Sergeyevich Prokofiev

Cinderella

Ballet in three acts. Libretto by Nikolai Volkov after the fairy tale by Charles Perrault.

Cinderella was first produced at the Bolshoi in 1945. It was choreographed by Rostislav Zakharov with set design by Pyotr Williams.

This ballet has been running for more than thirty years with constant success. The role of Cinderella has been danced by great Soviet ballerinas such as Olga Lepeshinskaya, Marina Semyonova, and Galina Ulanova, who have taken the ballet on many tours abroad, from Great Britain to Japan.

Opposite: Raisa S. Struchkova in the role of Cinderella. Top: M. B. Kondratyeva in another interpretation of Cinderella. Above left: M. L. Lavrovsky in the leading role, and once again Struchkova in the role of Cinderella. Above right: An extract from the ballet.

The subject of the fairy tale by Charles Perrault has inspired more than one composer with the idea of writing a ballet, but Prokofiev's Cinderella *is the one which, because of the melodious score with its touch of irony, has most of all inspired choreographers and performers.*

Above: Sketch by P. V. Williams (1902–47) for the 1945 production of Cinderella; *oil on canvas. Below: Sketch for the costumes for the ballet; oil on canvas, executed in 1945. Right: Scene of the ball in the Prince's palace. The role of Cinderella is performed by R. S. Struchkova.*

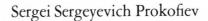

Sergei Sergeyevich Prokofiev

Romeo and Juliet

Ballet in three acts and thirteen scenes with a prologue and an epilogue. Libretto by Leonid Lavrovsky, Sergei Prokofiev, and Sergei Radlov after the tragedy by Shakespeare. First produced at the Bolshoi Theater in 1946, with choreography by Lavrovsky and set design by Pyotr Williams. Galina Ulanova danced an unsurpassable Juliet and the success of the ballet was such that it has become one of the classics of today. It is produced in many theaters throughout the world; in 1955 it was put on in a square in the city of Verona, on the very spot where Shakespeare's tragedy was set.

Above: N. I. Bessmertnova in the role of Juliet and M. L. Lavrovsky in the role of Romeo. Below: Ball scene. Opposite: A great dancer of the past, Galina Ulanova. It is certain that when composing Romeo and Juliet *Prokofiev had Ulanova in mind for the leading part.*

194

Above: Ball scene. I. O. Kandat in the role of the Capulets' mother and V. V. Golubin in that of the Capulets' father. Shakespeare's tragedy of the two lovers in Verona has inspired many composers and choreographers, but it was the Prokofiev-Lavrovsky version which without a doubt became the most popular.

Left, from top to bottom: Ball scene with M. V. Kondratyeva in the role of Juliet; detail from a dance scene; N. I. Bessmertnova in the role of Juliet with V. V. Romanenko as Count Paris, the youth who has been chosen by Juliet's parents to be her husband, and whom Juliet pretends to accept.

Above: Square scene. In one of the many brawls provoked by the incurable rivalry between the two great Veronese families, Mercutio, a friend of the Montagues, is slain by Tybalt, nephew of Lady Capulet. The people stare at the body in alarm. Romeo, who tried to prevent this from happening, must now avenge his death.

Top, from left to right: M. E. Liepa in the role of Romeo; quarrel scene between Tybalt and Mercutio; the first meeting of Romeo and Juliet as performed by M. M. Plisetskaya. Above: Final scene. Romeo, believing his loved one dead, poisons himself; when Juliet awakens from her drugged sleep and realizes what has happened, she stabs herself.

Aram Khachaturian

Spartacus

Ballet in three acts, twelve scenes, and nine monologues. Libretto by Nikolai Volkov, revised by Yuri Grigorovich.

Spartacus, the composer's greatest success, has appeared in various productions. The 1968 production, discussed in these pages, was choreographed by Yuri Grigorovich with set design by S. Virsaladze and followed two previous productions.

The ballet narrates the historic episode of the hero who led the revolt of the slaves and gladiators in first-century A.D. Rome, in which his name became the symbol of the lot of oppressed peoples, and the symbol of resistance against slavery and violence. The all-male dances play a predominant dramatic role in the ballet, and it is no accident that eminent dancers as Vladimir Vassiliev and Maris Liepa have become so strongly associated with it.

Spartacus has received the Lenin prize.

Above: The adagio with Phrygia and Spartacus; Yekaterina Maximova in the role of Phrygia and V. V. Vasiliev in that of Spartacus. Left: M. E. Liepa in the role of Crasso. Spartacus, carried to Rome by Crasso, enslaved with his wife Phrygia, manages to organize a revolt which, despite initial success, is later drowned in blood.

201

Above: The slave market from Act I; V. V. Vasiliev in the role of
Spartacus and Yekaterina Maximova in that of Phrygia.
Top: an orgy in Crasso's house (Act I) with V. M. Gordeyev as
Spartacus. Opposite: V. V. Vasiliev, famous for his virtuosity and
dynamism, in the role of Spartacus.

Above: M. L. Lavrovsky as Spartacus. Opposite, left, from top to bottom:
N. V. Timofeyeva in the role of Egina; S. D. Adyrchayeva in the role of
Egina. Opposite right: The last fight, from Act III. Run through with
lances, the body of Spartacus is raised as a sign of victory.

Arif Dzhanzhirovich Melikov

Legend of Love

Ballet in three acts. Libretto by Nazim Hikmet. *Legend of Love* appeared for the first time in the Bolshoi in 1965. It was choreographed by Yuri Grigorovich with set design by S. Virsaladze. In many respects this ballet is experimental, uniting dance and pantomime, classical and folk dancing, taking as its theme an ancient legend by the well-known Turkish poet and dramatist Nazim Hikmet. The ballet has the colour and feeling of ancient Persian miniatures.

Opposite, above: After the premiere the performers thank the audience for their warm applause. Opposite below: M. L. Lavrovsky in the role of Ferhad and N. V. Timofeyeva in that of Mehmene-Banu. Above: S. D. Adyrchayeva in the role of Mehmene-Banu, the queen who sacrifices her own beauty in order to save her sister Shiriene from a fatal illness..

Opposite, above: A scene from the ballet. Opposite, below: the finale.
Above: N. I. Bessmertnova in the role of Shiriene and M. L. Lavrovsky
in that of Ferhad, the painter who, in order to fulfill the task of
supplying water to the people who cannot get it, renounces his love for
Princess Shiriene and remains in the mountains searching for a new
spring.

Igor Fyodorovich Stravinsky

The Rite of Spring

Ballet in one act. Libretto by N. Kasatkina and Vladimir Vassiliev. Stravinsky subtitled his ballet *Scenes of Pagan Russia*.

First produced in Paris in 1913, the ballet was a failure, yet in a short time it was to become one of the mainstays of music and ballet in our century. It was produced at the Bolshoi Theater on June 28, 1964, under the direction of G. Rozhdestvensky, choreography by Natalya Kasatkina and Vladimir Vassiliev, set design by A. Goncharov.

Top: N. D. Kasatkina. Above: Scene from the ballet. Opposite: Y. K. Vladimirov supporting N. I. Sorokina, who is dancing the chosen maiden, the principal character in this fertility rite, which comes from the folklore of pagan Russia. In order for the wonders of spring to be repeated each year, the maiden must be sacrificed.

Vladimir Alexsandrovich Vlasov

Asel

Ballet in three acts made up of reminiscences. Libretto by B. Kaliyulov and N. Karitonov, after the story by the Soviet Kirghiz writer Chingiz Aitmatov. *Asel* was first produced at the Bolshoi Theater on February 7, 1967, with choreography by O. Vinogradov and set design by V. Leventhal. The choreographer managed to resolve difficult problems posed by the translation of the subject into classical dance by making great use of other means of expression. The rhythm, angularity of poses, and short, sharp movements are among the many characteristics that give this ballet its experimental air.

The libretto of Asel, *based on a story by Chingiz Aitmatov, relates the story of a truck driver who, having left his lady love (Asel) for a new love, comes back to find her happily married to a demobilized soldier. The three protagonists relate the story, each from his own point of view.*

Top: N. I. Sorokina in the role of Asel and B. B. Akimov in the role of Ilyasa. Above left: The recollection scene. Above right: B. B. Akimov again in the role of Ilyasa and N. I. Sorokina in the role of Asel. Opposite: Nina Ivanovna Sorokina in the costume of Asel, executing a perfect arabesque.

Top: Scene from Act I. Above: Still from Act I, the drivers' dance.
Opposite: Nina Vladimirovna Timofeyeva in the role of Asel. The
celebrated ballerina, who joined the Bolshoi in 1956, created an
unforgettable interpretation of this character.

Georges Bizet /
Rodion Konstantinovich Shchedrin

The Carmen Suite

Ballet in one act. Libretto by A. Alonzo, after the short
story by Prosper Mérimée.
The Bolshoi Theater premiere took place on April 20,
1967, with choreography by A. Alonzo and set design by
B. Messerer. It was the idea of the ballerina Maya
Plisetskaya to create a ballet to the famous music of
Carmen by Bizet. She turned to the Cuban choreographer
Alberto Alonzo with her idea, and a year later he brought
the libretto of a new ballet to Moscow. Alonzo attempts
to tell the story of the gypsy girl Carmen purely in the
language of choreography, to create a ballet to the
passionate and temperamental music of Bizet and
through this to create the character of Carmen.

Above: Sketch by B. A. Messerer for the 1967 production of The
Carmen Suite; *oil on canvas. Left: M. M. Plisetskaya in the role of
Carmen and A. A. Lavreniuk in that of the toreador. Opposite:
Maya Plisetskaya again, in the role of Carmen, with A. B. Godunov
in the role of José.*

217

Above: Maya Plisetskaya in the role of Carmen and S. N. Radchenko as Escamillo. Opposite left: M. M. Plisetskaya in the role of Carmen. Opposite right: Three extracts from the ballet performed by M. M. Plisetskaya in the role of Carmen and A. B. Godunov in the role of José.

On the following pages: Scene from The Carmen Suite *– a stylized arena, above which is a huge bull's head, the symbol of fate. The ballet, loosely based on the famous novel by Prosper Mérimée, relates a dramatic story in which Carmen, bound by fate, dies.*

218

Rodion Konstantinovich Shchedrin

Anna Karenina

Lyrical scenes, ballet in three acts. Libretto by B. Lvov-
Anokin, after the novel by Lev Tolstoy.
Anna Karenina was first produced at the Bolshoi
Theater on June 10, 1972. It was choreographed by
Maya Plisetskaya, N. Rizhenko, and V. Smirnov-
Golovanov. Set design by V. Leventhal.
The ballet marked the debut of Maya Plisetskaya as
choreographer; she also danced in the role of Anna.
The original language of ballet, the mastery and
artistic understanding make this ballet a great event in
the life of the Soviet theater. *Anna Karenina* is the first
ballet to be produced based on one of Tolstoy's works.

Opposite: Sketch by V. Y. Leventhal for the 1972 production of
Anna Karenina; *oil on canvas. Above: Ball scene. The plot of the*
ballet follows faithfully the main events narrated by Lev Tolstoy in
the novel of the same name, with the exception of the episode
concerning Levin and Kitty.

Top, from left to right: Maya Plisetskaya in the role of Anna, first with N. B. Fadeyechev in the role of Karenin and A. G. Boguslavskaya in the role of Betsy, then with M. E. Liepa as Karenin, and lastly A. B. Godunov as Vronsky. Above: Another sketch by Leventhal for the production of Anna Karenina.

Opposite: Plisetskaya as Anna. The costumes which the ballerina wears in this ballet were created by Pierre Cardin. Maya Plisetskaya, apart from being a dancer with exceptional technique and a fascinating cinema actress, proved herself to be, in Anna Karenina, *an able choreographer.*

Left: Scene at the horse races. Top: Plisetskaya with an enormous ostrich-feather fan, performing the role of Anna Karenina in the scene which takes place in a theater. Above: The journey into Italy; Plisetskaya in the role of Anna, with A. B. Godunov in the role of her lover, Count Vronsky.

Ivan the Terrible

Ballet in two acts. Libretto by Yuri Grigorovich.
In the forties, Prokofiev wrote the music for
Eisenstein's film *Ivan the Terrible*. The leading
choreographer with the Bolshoi, Yuri Grigorovich,
with the help of M. Chulaki, used the score to create a
ballet about the ferocious and bloody life of Russia in
the sixteenth century under the reign of Ivan IV,
during which, in spite of the rebellion of the boyars,
wars, and raids by neighbouring peoples, the Russian
state was formed and consolidated. The ballet was first
produced in the Bolshoi Theater in 1975, with
choreography by Yuri Grigorovich, set design by S.
Virsaladze as illustrated in these pages.

*Above: N. I. Bessmertnova in the role of Anastasia and Y. K.
Vladimirov in that of Ivan IV. Right: The poisoning of Tsarina
Anastasia plotted by the boyars. Opposite: Natalia Igoryevna
Bessmertnova in the role of Anastasia and Vladimir Viktorovich
Vasiliev as Ivan IV.*

Above: The bell ringers' scene from Act I. The ballet, while illustrating the complex personality of Ivan IV, does not claim to reproduce exactly the era, but nevertheless illustrates its philosophy and its atmosphere. The theme is the formation of the Russian national character, the consolidation of the traditions of honesty and heroism. On the following pages: The throne room, with Ivan and the boyars.

230

Top, from left to right: N. I. Bessmertnova in the role of Anastasia and Y. K. Vladimirov in the role of Ivan; B. B. Akimov in the role of the treacherous boyar Kurbsky and Bessmertnova in that of Anastasia. Above: scene from Act II, Y. K. Vladimirov in the role of Ivan and Bessmertnova in that of Anastasia. Opposite: The finale of the ballet. Ivan IV, seizing the bell ropes (the bells are ringing out, calling the Russian people to unite), subdues his people.

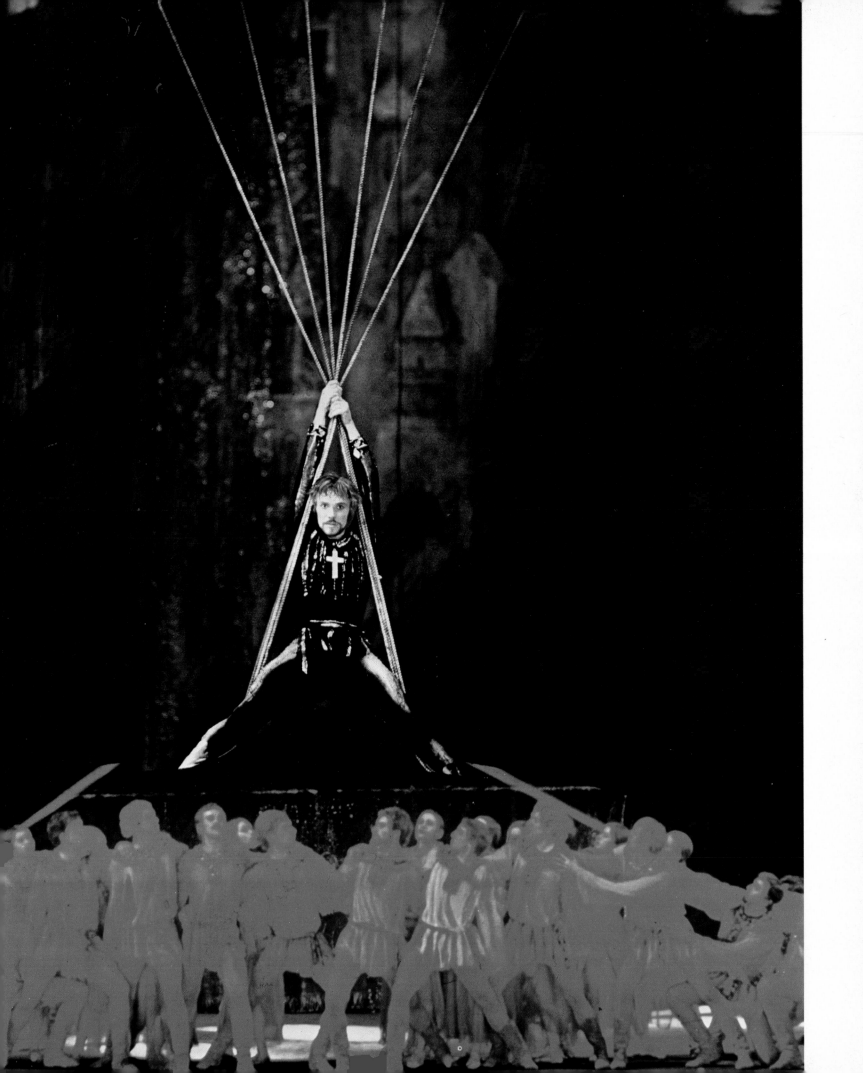

Repertoire of the Bolshoi Theater

OPERAS

M. Glinka. *Ivan Susanin.* First given 1842. Ten productions in all. Last version produced 1945.

M. Glinka. *Russlan and Ludmilla.* First given 1846. Ten productions in all. Last version produced 1972.

A. Dargomizhsky. *Rusalka.* First given 1859. Seven productions in all. Last version produced 1976.

G. Verdi. *Il Trovatore.* First given 1859. Four productions in all. Last version produced 1972.

C. Gounod. *Faust.* First given 1866. Six productions in all. Last version produced 1969.

G. Verdi. *La Traviata.* First given 1872. Nine productions in all. Last version produced 1953.

G. Verdi. *Don Carlos.* First given 1876. Three productions in all. Last version produced 1963.

G. Verdi. *Aida.* First given 1879. Seven productions in all. Last version produced 1951.

G. Verdi. *Rigoletto.* First given 1879. Eight productions in all. Last version produced 1963.

P. Tchaikovsky. *Eugene Onegin.* First given 1881. Eight productions in all. Last version produced 1944.

G. Rossini. *The Barber of Seville.* First given 1883. Ten productions in all. Last version produced 1965.

M. Mussorgsky. *Boris Godunov.* First given 1888. Five productions in all. Last version produced 1948.

P. Tchaikovsky. *The Queen of Spades.* First given 1891. Nine productions in all. Last version produced 1964.

G. Verdi. *Othello.* First given 1891. Three productions in all. Last version produced 1978.

P. Tchaikovsky. *Iolanthe.* First given 1893. Five productions in all. Last version produced 1974.

N. Rimsky-Korsakov. *Snow Maiden.* First given 1893. Six productions in all. Last version given 1978.

A. Borodin. *Prince Igor.* First given 1898. Six productions in all. Last version produced 1953.

G. Bizet. *Carmen.* First given 1898. Six productions in all. Last version produced 1953.

N. Rimsky-Korsakov. *The Maid of Pskov (Ivan the Terrible).* First given 1901. Three productions in all. Last version produced in 1971.

N. Rimsky-Korsakov. *Mozart and Salieri.* First given 1901. Three productions in all. Last version produced 1977.

S. Rachmaninov. *Francesca da Rimini.* First given 1906. Two productions in all. Last version produced 1956.

A. Dargomizhsky. *The Stone Guest.* First given 1906. Two productions in all. Last version produced 1976.

N. Rimsky-Korsakov. *Sadko.* First given 1906. Four productions in all. Last version produced 1949.

N. Rimsky-Korsakov. *Legend of the Invisible City of Kitezh.* First given 1908. Five productions in all. Last version produced 1966.

M. Mussorgsky. *Khovanshchina (The Khovansky Affair).* First given 1912. Four productions in all. Last version produced 1950.

N. Rimsky-Korsakov. *The Tsar's Bride.* First given 1916. Six productions in all. Last version produced 1966.

G. Puccini. *Madama Butterfly.* First given 1925. Three productions in all. Last version produced 1966.

W. A. Mozart. *The Marriage of Figaro.* First given 1926. Three productions in all. Last version produced 1956.

G. Puccini. *Tosca.* First produced 1930. Five productions in all. Last version produced 1971.

S. Prokofiev. *War and Peace.* First given 1959.

V. Muradeli. *October.* First given 1964.

A. Kholminov. *An Optimistic Tragedy.* First given 1967.

K. Molchanov. *The Unknown Soldier.* First given 1967.

M. Pauchwerger. *The Snow Queen.* First given 1969.

S. Prokofiev. *Semyon Kotko.* First given 1970.

S. Prokofiev. *The Gambler.* First given 1974.

K. Molchanov. *Here the Dawn Is Quiet.* First given 1975.

R. Shchedrin. *Dead Souls.* First given 1977.

O. Taktakishvili. *The Abduction of the Moon.* First given 1977.

M. Ravel. *L'Heure Espagnole.* First given 1978.

W. A. Mozart. *Così Fan Tutte.* First given 1978.

B. Bartók. *Duke Bluebeard's Castle.* First given 1978.

BALLETS

A. Adam. *Giselle.* First given 1843. Nine productions in all. Last version produced 1944.

L. Minkus. *Don Quixote.* First given 1869. Four productions in all. Last version produced 1940.

P. Tchaikovsky. *Swan Lake.* First given 1877. Eight productions in all. Last version produced 1969.

P. Tchaikovsky. *Sleeping Beauty.* First given 1899. Seven productions in all. Last version produced 1973.

A. K. Glazunov. *Raymonda.* First given 1900. Three productions in all. Last version produced 1945.

L. Minkus. *Kingdom of Shades.* (From *La Bayadere*). First given 1904. Three productions in all. Last version produced 1977.

P. Tchaikovsky. *The Nutcracker.* First given 1919. Four productions in all. Last version produced 1966.

R. M. Glière. *The Red Poppy.* First given 1927. Three productions in all. Last version produced 1957.

F. Chopin. *Chopiniana (Les Sylphides).* First given 1932. Five productions in all. Last version produced 1958.

B. Asafiev. *The Fountain of Bakhchisarai.* First given 1936.

S. Prokofiev. *Cinderella.* First given 1945.

S. Prokofiev. *Romeo and Juliet.* First given 1946.

S. Prokofiev. *The Stone Flower.* First given 1954. Two productions in all. Last version produced 1959.

A. Khachaturian. *Spartacus.* First given 1958. Three productions in all. Last version produced 1968.

R. Shchedrin. *The Humpbacked Horse.* First given 1960.

S. Rachmaninov. *Paganini.* First given 1960.

N. Karetnikov. *Geologists.* First given 1964.

A. Melikov. *The Legend of Love.* First given 1965.

I. Stravinsky. *The Rite of Spring.* First given 1965.

V. Vlasov. *Asel.* First given 1967.

G. Bizet and R. Shchedrin. *The Carmen Suite.* First given 1967.

S. Slonimsky. *Icarus.* First given 1971. Two productions in all. Last version produced 1976.

R. Shchedrin. *Anna Karenina.* First given 1972.

G. Mahler. *La Rose Malade.* First given 1973.

W. A. Mozart and A. Salieri. *Mozart and Salieri.* First given 1973.

A. Pakhmutov. *Brilliance.* First given 1974.

S. Prokofiev. *Ivan the Terrible.* First given 1975.

T. Khrennikov. *Much Ado About Nothing.* First Given 1976.

A. Eshpai. *Angara.* First given 1976.

K. Khachaturian. *Cipollino.* First given 1977.

E. Svetlanov. *Kalina Krasnaya (The Red Guelder Rose).* First given 1978.

A. Corelli, G. Torelli, J.-P. Rameau, W.A. Mozart. *These Enchanting Sounds.* First given 1978.

THE BOLSHOI THEATER COMPANY'S TOURS

Since 1945, the Bolshoi Ballet and Opera companies have gone on tour to the following countries: Argentina, Australia, Austria, Belgium, Brazil, Bulgaria, Burma, Canada, China, Cuba, Czechoslovakia, Denmark, Egypt, Finland, France, Federal Republic of Germany, German Democratic Republic, Great Britain, Greece, Hungary, India, Ireland, Italy, Japan, Lebanon, Libya, Mexico, Netherlands, New Zealand, Norway, Philippines, Poland, Rumania, Sweden, Switzerland, Syria, Tunisia, United States of America, Uruguay, Yugoslavia.

The operas given on tour are the following: *Here the Dawn Is Quiet, Boris, Godunov, The Queen of Spades, Eugene Onegin, The Gambler, War and Peace, Khovanshchina, The Legend of the Invisible City of Kitezh, Prince Igor, Russlan and Ludmilla, Sadko, Semyon Kotko, The Unknown Soldier, Tosca.*

The ballets given on tour are the following: *Anna Karenina, Sleeping Beauty, Bolero, The Carmen Suite, The Bronze Horseman, The Humpbacked Horse, Cinderella, Chopiniana (Les Sylphides), Classical Concert, Coppelia, Divertissement, Don Quixote, The Stone Flower, The Fountain of Bakhchisarai, Gayane, Giselle, Ivan the Terrible, Swan Lake, Legend of Love, Mirandolina, Walpurgis Night, Paganini, Path of Thunder, Preludes and Fugues, Romeo and Juliet, La Rose Malade, The Rite of Spring, The Nutcracker, Scriabiniana, Lieutenant Kizhe, Spartacus, Dance Suite, Le Spectre de la Rose.*

The Bolshoi orchestra and the Bolshoi choir have also given separate performances.

Index of Operas and Ballets

OPERAS

BALLETS